Crichton

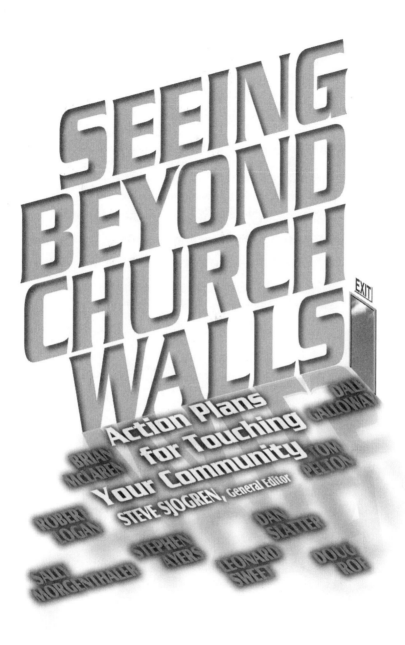

SEEING BEYOND CHURCH WALLS

Action Plans for Touching Your Community

STEVE SJOGREN, General Editor

DAN GALLOWAY

BRIAN McLAREN

TOM PELTON

ROBERT LOGAN

DAN SLATTER

SALLY MORGENTHALER

STEPHEN AYERS

LEONARD SWEET

DOUG ROE

Flagship church resources

from Group Publishing

SEEING BEYOND CHURCH WALLS
ACTION PLANS FOR TOUCHING YOUR COMMUNITY

Visit our Web site: **www.grouppublishing.com**

CREDITS
Authors: Steve Sjogren, Brian D. McLaren, Tom Pelton, Stephen
    L. Ayers, Doug Roe, Sally Morgenthaler, Dale E. Galloway,
    Dan Slatter, Robert E. Logan, and Leonard Sweet
Senior Editor: Paul Woods
Chief Creative Officer: Joani Schultz
Assistant Editor: Alison Imbriaco
Book Designer: Jean Bruns
Computer Graphic Artist: Nancy Serbus
Cover Art Director: Jeff A. Storm
Cover Designer: Alan Furst, Inc.
Production Manager: Peggy Naylor

Unless otherwise noted, Scripture taken from the HOLY BIBLE, NEW INTERNATIONAL VERSION®. Copyright © 1973, 1978, 1984 by International Bible Society. Used by permission of Zondervan Publishing House. All rights reserved.

LIBRARY OF CONGRESS CATALOGING-IN-PUBLICATION DATA
Seeing beyond church walls : action plan for touching your
community / by Steve Sjogren, general editor.
        p. cm.
    Includes bibliographical references.
    ISBN 0-7644-2343-6 (alk. paper)
    1. Community--Religious aspects--Christianity. 2. Church
    work. I. Sjogren, Steve, 1955-

BV625 .S44 2001
253--dc21   2001054314

10 9 8 7 6 5 4 3 2 1   10 09 08 07 06 05 04 03 02

Printed in the United States of America.

CONTENTS

Introduction

THE WAY OF THE WAY OUT

BY
STEVE
SJOGREN

"BUT I THOUGHT WE *WERE* OUTWARD-FOCUSED..."

Most churches are struggling with survival issues. For many, just staying in business financially or getting beyond a sense of defeat is the topic at hand. The average church is, by emotional and organizational default, inwardly focused. Perhaps because we have lacked a clear model for looking outward, the standard for conducting business in the church makes it nearly impossible to see beyond our church walls.

This book is a *booster rocket* for those whose visionary tails are dragging. It's a *mind expander* for those who have not adequately thought through their outward direction. I hope you will find it full of paradigm adjustments.

Through this book, ten encouraging voices speak to those who are discouraged to the point of just hanging in there and praying for a breakthrough from God. The authors write, not as the highly gifted or the "arrived" experts, but as fellow strugglers who have discovered enduring truths.

This is an important book because there aren't many churches in the world that are truly outward-focused as defined in this book. I honestly think that churches truly architected to be outward-focused are a rarity. On the other hand, whenever I speak or write on this topic, people come out of the woodwork to say, essentially, "That's what we desperately need to become. Can you help us—*please?*"

Here you have our attempt to help you build a church that truly sees beyond its walls.

LET'S GET PRACTICAL

One of the surprising best-selling books of recent years is *The Worst-Case Scenario Survival Handbook,* by Joshua Piven and David Borgenicht. How can it not be a hit? Consider its chapters: "How to Jump From a Building Into a Dumpster" and "How to Survive If Your Parachute Fails to Open." I've actually used "How to Escape From Killer Bees." (Well, they weren't actually killer bees, but they stung just the same). The one I hope I will never have to use is "How to Wrestle From an Alligator." (I probably won't have to worry about that in Cincinnati because our alligators are so polite they'd ask permission before they bite.)[1]

One of the more darkly funny worst-case-scenario lists is compiled by Thrifty Car Rental. According to PR Newswire, entries in Thrifty's annual Honeymoon Disaster contest describe run-ins with hurricanes, watching a cruise ship leave without the honeymoon couple, and being arrested in Mexico.

For Debbie and Steve Meyer of Sudbury, Massachusetts, winners of the contest, the problems began before the honeymoon had officially started. They flew to Maui prior to the wedding and went to what was supposed to be their honeymoon hideaway. What they found was less than appealing. Not only was the place a mess, the renters who had abused it were still there—and in no hurry to leave! The PR Newswire story recounts that, "after playing bellhops to the interlopers and helping them out with their bags, the Meyers discovered a paradise of unmade beds, grimy floors, greasy pans, and refrigerators growing science experiments."

When the hideaway was finally empty, the Meyers realized that it was time to get ready for the wedding. They hurriedly searched for towels, but not a towel was to be found. "They called the owner who returned with towels, which he proceeded to shake and sniff. 'I think this one's clean,' he said, handing one to the bride-to-be.

The Meyers fled.

Fortunately, they stumbled onto an available condo and, just twenty minutes before the wedding, began to shower and dress for the wedding. Apparently they didn't mind meeting the minister with wet hair, but Debbie realized she had forgotten her shoes. The couple rushed back to the condo for the shoes and returned to the church—which they found locked. Unwilling to give up, the couple had an impromptu outdoor wedding in a graveyard next to the church. It rained, of course.

The next morning, the minister informed the Meyers that their wedding adventure wasn't over. Due to a technicality, they weren't really married. The couple quickly signed the necessary papers and left for a quiet, private hike in the rainforest. The Meyers found a steep climb, beautiful scenery, and, suddenly, a scream. Before the day was over, they were enlisted by rescue personnel to help find someone who had fallen from a rocky cliff.

Then, when the Meyers finally returned to the condo, they found it completely enclosed in a giant tent for insect fumigation.[2]

Whether we realize it or not, the church is facing an all-too-serious set of worst-case scenarios. The scenarios are far more critical than an alligator bite or a bad honeymoon. We are facing ultimate survival issues. While we all know the truth of the verse, "I will build my church, and the gates of Hades will not overcome it" (Matthew 16:18b), the real question today is, will the church survive another generation of its own inwardly focused gaze? We are looking at missing out on the very purpose for which God created the church—which is to be an outward-facing force connecting with the not-yet-Christians of this world whom Jesus so loved that he died for them. He has in mind for us to be the ultimate all-inclusive family. Unfortunately, more often than not, we more closely resemble the Addams family.

> In "A Treatise Concerning the Properties and Effects of Coffee," written in 1785, Dr. Benjamin Mosely included endorsements from names we still recognize. "[Sir Francis] Bacon said, 'Coffee comforts the head and heart, and helps digestion.' Dr. Willis says, 'being drank daily, it wonderfully clears and enlightens each part of the soul, and disperses all the clouds of every function'...Voltaire almost lived on it; and the learned and sedentary of every country have recourse to it, to refresh the brain oppressed by study and contemplation."[3]

A CALL TO ACTION

We need to take action.

I've been a coffee drinker for years. I enjoy the smell, the taste, the look—the entire experience of coffee. I'm a raving fan of the drink.

Maybe the church as a whole needs to drink more coffee to get motivated. It's good at getting us going.

But we need more than coffee to do what is discussed in

these pages. We need the power of the Holy Spirit continually upon us and on what we are stepping out to do. In Norwegian, the word for coffee "bean" is the same as the word for "prayer" ("bønne"). That coincidence makes perfect sense to me. At the root of our success in the outward-focused church is the need for stimulation from beyond us. Coffee helps. Prayer and the empowering of the Spirit are essential.

He is ready, willing, and enthusiastic about filling us with his power to change the world.

Steve Sjogren,
ssjogren@one.net
www.servantevangelism.com

Veni, Vedi, Velcro
"I came, I saw, I stuck around"

ENDNOTES

1. Joshua Piven and David Borgenicht, *The Worst-Case Scenario Survival Handbook* (San Francisco: Chronicle Books, 1999).

2. " 'Goldilocks' Hard Luck Story Wins Thrifty Car Rental's Honeymoon Disasters Contest," PR Newswire (14 February, 2001).

3. Benjamin Moseley, M.D., "A Treatise Concerning the Properties and Effects of Coffee," 1785.

SIMPLY PROFOUND CHRISTIANITY

Loving Those Beyond Church Walls

BY STEVE SJOGREN

ast year Christmas Eve fell on a Sunday night. Sometimes, after a weekend of services (at Vineyard Community Church, we have five identical services), I wonder if we don't do church too much. I worry about the children of our church one day coming to the conclusion: Jesus I love—it's church I can't stand. So we announced that we were calling off Christmas Eve services. The response wasn't positive. There were lots of moans from the crowd, and e-mail protests flooded our offices.

We came up with Plan B. We announced that on Christmas Eve we would gather, sing a couple of carols, then go out into the community to minister to all those who have to work that night by serving them Krispy Kreme donuts. That idea was better received. We bought eight thousand donuts (the really good kind) so that we could distribute donuts, Christmas carols, and brief prayers of blessing to all who were stuck working on Christmas Eve.

At the end of our brief Christmas Eve service, hundreds of carloads of people and their donuts sped toward firehouses, police stations, and restaurants.

One group went to a local, twenty-four-hour restaurant that specializes in waffles. As they walked in, the Vineyard people couldn't help but notice that everyone in the place was unhappy about being there. The employees were unhappy because they were stuck working when they wanted to be home with their families. The customers were unhappy because they were sufficiently distanced or ostracized from their families that they were eating waffles alone on this most family-focused night of the year.

The group had its work cut out for it, so two teams were formed. Several individuals approached the manager and offered to show him the love of Christ by taking over the dishwashing duties for a couple of hours. The manager said, "Well, no one has ever volunteered to do that. The boss isn't going to come in tonight of all times…Sure!"

The other church people went to work on improving the atmosphere in the restaurant. Fortunately the jukebox offered the tunes of Motown diva Miss Diana Ross. Our people started to dance. And they danced. For two hours, they danced. They asked the folks sitting alone at their tables eating their eggs and waffles to please dance with them.

Now, I realize that some reading this might take offense at the notion of Christians dancing; but the way I look at it, there's a time and a place and a way to dance, just as there is a time and place to not dance. This was surely a time to dance. Most of the invitees refused to hoof it...at least at first. "I can't dance," they said. "I'm no good!"

"That's OK, neither are we," said the dancers. "We're just having some fun." Before long the entire restaurant looked like the African-American church scene in *The Blues Brothers* movie—almost *everyone* was dancing, even some of the workers.

The party lasted a couple of hours. As the group departed, everyone in the restaurant called, "Goodbye, you Vineyard folks!"

I thought the story was over when I heard about it a couple of days after Christmas. Then, about a week later, a psychiatrist called the church. He said that he couldn't reveal their names, but oddly, two of his clients came to see him that week. Though the patients didn't know each other, they both happened to be in the same restaurant at the same time. This doctor fully expected to hear about horrible experiences of loneliness at Christmas. Instead, he was told about being encouraged to dance to the tunes of Diana Ross by some semi-crazy Christians.

"May I ask you a question?" the psychiatrist asked. "Do you worship to Diana Ross songs at your weekend celebrations as well?"

All I could think to say was, "Not yet."

That outreach on Christmas Eve wasn't about Diana Ross, waffles, or washing dishes,

> That night, for a brief while, the church was doing what Christ had in mind from the beginning—that, through his people, he would build an atmosphere that made it easier to move toward the healing power of Christ than to stay away from him.

though they came together to build an atmosphere. That night, for a brief while, the church was doing what Christ had in mind from the beginning—that, through his people, he would build an atmosphere that would make it easier to move toward the healing power of Christ than to stay away from him.

BIG HEART

Jesus spelled out in the clearest of language what the church is to be all about:

> " 'Love the Lord your God with all your heart
> and with all your soul and with all your mind.'
> This is the first and greatest commandment. And the
> second is like it: 'Love your neighbor as yourself' "
> (Matthew 22:37-39).

The Bible is clear; it provides a mandate. God wants his church to see outside its walls. He has in mind a church that would be ever-increasing in heart and size. If we go back to the original outward-calling document, the Great Commission, Jesus gets down to the simple elements of his heart:

> "All authority in heaven and on earth has been
> given to me. So wherever you go, make disciples of
> all nations: Baptize them in the name of the Father,
> and of the Son, and of the Holy Spirit. Teach them
> to do everything I have commanded you.
> "And remember that I am always with you
> until the end of time" (Matthew 28:18-20, God's
> Word Version).

What stands out in these lines is how many times Jesus alludes to the concept of inclusion. He says, essentially, "*All* the resources needed have been given to me, so I want *all* of you, to go to *all* people groups, to teach them *all* my message, by *all* means available to you, and I will be with you *all* the time as you do this." Again and again Jesus says or implies *all.* He does it so often there is no way we could possibly miss the all-inclusiveness of his heart.

Obviously Jesus was trying to get a point across loud and clear. His message is, "My family can't be large enough to satisfy my heart. My heart is larger than you, the church, or even the human race can comprehend. It is unlimited in its ability to include all who call on the name of Christ."

As a child, I entered a kite-flying contest and won in the Largest to Fly category. It was a Jolly Green Giant kite. I received it in the mail, a reward for eating my vegetables and sending in the ends of frozen peas boxes. The thing was enormous. Over six feet tall, it was about two feet taller than me at that age! On a blustery day, the wind resistance was so great it took two friends and me to hold onto it once it was airborne. It wore us out after half an hour of flying. The experience of flying it was so tiring that I flew it just once— in that contest.

God's heart is Jolly-Green-Giant-size and then some—to the thousandth power! God is all about including. The practical problem God has is on the human side of the equation. We humans struggle with issues of accepting people who are different from us. The vast majority of people in the church say, "Diversity, YES!" But it takes a lot of plain hard work and expending of energy to truly embrace diversity.

We find it stressful to relate to outsiders who dress differently, whose bodies are pierced in more places than ours are, or who have more tattoos than we do. It takes indescribable energy to hang on to the kite string and manage the resistance that comes with flying that kite of big-time inclusiveness that comes close to resembling the heart of God. But the difficulties we encounter don't change the heart of God one bit. God is still absolutely, totally, perfectly inclusive.

When he said, "I want *all* of you to go into *all* of the world to bring them *all* into my family," he was speaking measured words. They were his last words to his disciples.

As humans we can't understand this message because we automatically think in terms of limitations. We do a bit of ministry—if we're gifted and anointed by God, perhaps we do a lot of ministry. But we all get tired.

When Jesus gave the Great Commission, he had in mind a family that could never be large enough to satisfy his inclusive heart. Unfortunately more often than not we've experienced the *great omission*. While not all churches are called to be large, we are all called to be growing. We are all called to have a dynamic relationship with our surrounding communities.

This idea of being inclusive in ever-increasing ways is impossible for us to wrap our minds around. We step out to love the unlovely, and we find that it's stressful stuff to love those who are different from us. We grow tired. It's human nature to grow weary or even give up. That's why Paul says in Galatians 6:9a, "Let us not become weary in doing good." It is human nature to grow weary.

HEART FOR THE SIMPLE

We've made evangelism the most complicated ministry in the church instead of what Jesus had in mind—that it be the simplest one. Outreach is the only thing a person who is brand new in a relationship with Christ can do to benefit God's kingdom within minutes of coming to faith in Jesus.

Think about it.

As soon as we make a faith commitment, we can begin to tell people about what God has started in our hearts. A new follower of Christ has no formal training but is instantly equipped to share his or her testimony.

That's exactly what I began to do when, as a college freshman, I rather suddenly came to know Christ. No one had trained me in the fine art of evangelism. In fact, no one had officially "led me to the Lord." I was simply curious and began to read the four Gospels.

I had actually gone to a Doobie Brothers concert and heard them sing "Jesus Is Just Alright." As I look back now, I realize I had a "God encounter" at that "secular" concert. (The concert was held in Tempe, Arizona's Sun Devil stadium, no less! Go figure.) Out of nowhere, a thought planted itself in my head that night: *Every well-rounded, educated person ought to read the Bible at least once in life.*

Not knowing any better, I picked up the Gospel of Matthew and read...and began to fall in love with the person of Jesus. I read through Mark, Luke, and John and was hooked on the Doobie Brothers' message. For some reason, I skipped Acts and went right into Romans—a fatal mistake for anyone trying to avoid a conversion experience. I got to chapter 8 and realized the lost condition of my life. Suddenly I knew that I needed a redeemer to bring me desperately needed direction.

I remember praying my own homespun "sinner's prayer" during the evening I put Romans 8 together with the Gospels. Since no one had coached me and I had never read the Four Spiritual Laws tract, I made up my own prayer. *"Well God, here I am."* That little prayer expressed the simple trust I had in my heart, the ultimate surrender I was making. Though it was short and sweet, I think I said it all.

It wasn't until some weeks later that a "more mature" believer informed me that I hadn't really prayed to receive Christ because I had missed several key theological elements…blah, blah, blah. So I received Christ again, mostly to make him happy. But I knew in my heart that my first prayer had captured the heart of it all—"Well, God, here I am."

I've been doing some study in Scripture since that encounter. It is remarkable how many major characters prayed the "Here I am" prayer at a major turning point in their relationship with God. Moses and Aaron did. David did more than once. Isaiah prayed that prayer as he went into prophetic ministry.

I've been informally polling Christians around the world, asking them what they prayed to receive Christ. I've asked people on many continents the same question. Usually the first answer is a fine-sounding, King James-ish prayer. Then I ask, "No, what did you pray before that—when you were alone, in the shower, in bed before going to sleep, driving to work—you remember, *that* prayer." They almost always say, "Oh, that's when I prayed, 'God, here I am…' " We start out simple. The environment of the church world is what makes us increasingly complex.

THERE'S MORE WE CAN DO THAN JUST PRAY FOR THEM, SISTER

One of the memorable comedy films of the '90s was

Sister Act. You probably remember "Sister" Whoopi Goldberg (Deloris Van Cartier/Sister Mary Clarence) from the Reno convent. After introducing the radical idea of singing songs with a little bit of beat to them and singing the words in English instead of Latin, the good sister was reamed out by the Mother Superior behind closed doors.

"What next, boogie-woogie in the sanctuary?…That's it! You're fired from leading the choir." At that moment, the priest stopped by to offer his praise for the wonderful music the new sister had introduced. The rest of the sisters found their way into the office and shared their spontaneous opinions about the direction of the convent.

Whoopi said (without permission), "Not only are we going to change the music a little, but the good sister wants us to go out and meet the neighborhood!"

The sisters cheered with excitement.

My favorite sister is Mary Lazarus (Mary Wickes). (She was the one with the squeaky voice and the hearing aid hung around her neck.) She chimed in with the profound line, "You know sister, there's a lot more we can do than just pray for them."

I suspect the writers of *Sister Act* weren't aware of how biblical they were being at the time, but they put together a cast of nuns who would live out the truth of Hebrews 10:24.

"Think of ways to encourage one another to outbursts of love and good deeds" (Hebrews 10:24, New Living Translation).

The Living Bible goes further by using the words, *"Let us outdo each other."* In other words, the verse is a call to a kindness competition!

"Let us outdo each other in being helpful and kind to each other and in doing good" (Hebrews 10:24b, The Living Bible).

By putting the two readings together, we come up with something like this: "Let us outdo one another in our outbursts of love and good deeds!" That draws a picture of nearly out-of-control levels of kindness, unselfishness, generosity, and compassion. What a vision for the church! Wouldn't it be exciting if the church became so spontaneous and outward that observers would comment, "Look, another outburst of love and good deeds."

And then, noticing the act would spark a healthy competition in the heart of another Christian, who would determine to figure out a way to be even more loving and full of good deeds—all to the glory of Christ. That sort of imagery is difficult (to the point of nearly impossible) to grasp, but that's what God has had in mind for his church from the beginning.

Sister Mary Lazarus was right—"there's a lot more we can do than just pray for them."

Recently I read about some for-real *Sister Act*-hearted nuns. According to an article in The Washington Post, these nuns could be found at Roberts Brothers Circus, past the man who eats fire and past The Skull, billed as "The Strangest Thing You'll Ever See."

Strange as the shrunken head might be, though, the new circus employees are equally fascinating. After all, how often will you see two Catholic missionary nuns, both in their fifties, who have joined the traveling circus? But Sister Dorothy Fabritze and Sister Bernard Overkamp, both of the Missionary Sisters of the Sacred Heart are too busy to think about being strange. They're selling and taking tickets, feeding the troupe's forty people, and ministering to the troupe's spiritual needs.

So why would two middle-aged nuns "run away" to join a traveling circus? Returning to this country after two decades of missionary work in Papua, New Guinea, the sisters felt little connection with the "consumer culture" they found at home. In the circus, they found a community—a community that needs them.

Sisters Dorothy and Bernard are part of a fledgling effort by a few Catholic nuns, in two religious orders, who have taken circus jobs as a means to offer spiritual assistance to those in the big top. They're traveling with the Roberts Brothers Circus, as Sister Dorothy said, to "let people in this circus know that there's a God who cares about them no matter what's happened in their lives."

To accomplish this, Sisters Dorothy and Bernard travel in a new trailer in which the two women pray daily and offer communion to interested circus employees. "So far," according to The Washington Post, "only three workers have taken communion at the little altar. But it's early, Sister Dorothy says…"You feel satisfied in this work if you can help even a few people find peace…even one.' "[1]

MISSION—THE ONE LITTLE THING

In the film *City Slickers*, Curly (Jack Palance), a veteran cowhand, mesmerizes the big-city businessmen who have come for a dude ranch experience. Of course, the city slickers get more than they bargain for in their week away. But the head cowboy, Curly, blows them away. One night, while sitting around the campfire like a bunch of little boys, someone asks the larger-than-life figure, "Curly, what's the secret to life?"

As he rolls a cigarette, Curly stretches out his index finger. "Just this."

"Your finger is the secret of life?"

"No, the one thing. The one thing that you are about—the one thing each of you has to figure out for yourself—that's the secret to life."

Curly was referring to what modern business vernacular would call a mission statement. For a church, it is a declaration that rallies the troops to passionate followership and unifies a group's focus. It's one part a call to war—not a call to just a support position, but to the front lines.

It's also one part poetry that gives laser-like clarification. It's a declaration for all the world to see and understand, and, more than anything, it's a definition of success.

Jesus summarized his mission with clarity that even Curly would envy. Roughly paraphrased, the mission is: "Love God. Love people. The rest is details" (Matthew 22:37-39).

Being the Church

In *The Essence of the Church*, Craig Van Gelder wrote that national attention had been focused on getting ready for the "next" church, "where the key to success will be functional ministry that is culturally relevant and organizationally sound." Van Gelder argued that, "rather than trying to find the 'next' church that will help us be successful one more time, we need to rediscover something more basic about what it means *to be* the church."[2]

Every time I speak at Vineyard Community Church, I come to a point in the message when I ask people to repeat our mission statement. I often have people close their eyes and say it together as if it were the pledge of allegiance. People cry every time. Why every week? Because it takes about six days to forget why we exist, why we are even getting together as a church, and what's the point of us doing all of this.

That need for simplicity stands in stark contrast to the specialization that has swept through the church in recent decades. Today's "bio churches" are known for their promise to produce life based on a program. These are the hyphenated churches. The seeker-targeted, purpose-driven, spirit-empowered, revival-expecting, _____-churches. Hyphenated churches sound good to people who are desperate for something to happen. Today, when the average weekend attendance is reported to be ninety adults[3], that sense of desperately seeking *something* is understandable.

In the absence of knowing what we are all about, we will continually be seeking the next new thing in church life. That's no way to conduct our spiritual lives.

I'm no fan of the fill-in-the-blank church model. For one thing, the older I get, the simpler I seem to become and the more skeptical I grow of complexity. Secondly, after pastoring for twenty-five years, I've been through my fair share of attempts to define *church* in a hyphenated manner. I've tried, without sustained fruit, to lead the prayer-teaching church, the prophesy-driven church, the power-of-the-Spirit church, the gifts-of-the-Spirit church, the church-growth church, and the power-evangelism church. The list goes on.

It's actually a bit depressing for me to write this because I am forced to reflect on my years of marginal effectiveness

> ## *Church of Whatever*
>
> In an editorial piece about the faith-based initiative, James Farinet wrote about a "conversation" with his "friend" Clive. A man critical of faith-based initiatives, Clive thinks churches are going to compromise themselves and become whatever it takes to get money and attract people. He says, "My church, 'The Church of the Whatever,' is talking about getting a grant for a marketing program to attract people. Now is that fair?"[4]

> *"Yes, we had a mission statement; what we lacked was a mission."*
>
> —Richard L. Dunagin[5]

as I attempted to do something effective for God. Similar to my conversion to Christ, I started out going to Sunday school as a small child carrying a simple white Bible with a brass zipper, but that approach to spirituality seemed all too simple to me. Even though it was right under my nose, I knew it wasn't possibly the "enlightened way" so I searched hither and yon in the spiritual world and read broadly. I searched in theology and philosophy.

I've come to resonate with the words of Jesus: Love God, love people.

I've been collecting stories from people who have done outlandish, distracting things while they were driving. To date some of the better ones I've received include the following:

- eating cereal while driving to school
- playing the flute while driving on a Los Angeles freeway (He steered with his elbows.)

But the best was in good conservative ol' Cincinnati. A friend observed a lady 1) talking on her cell phone, 2) eating a breakfast sandwich, and 3) breast-feeding her baby—all while driving in the high-speed lane.[7]

I have struggled with what to call this simpler sort of church.

It disturbs me that we live in such a time that we have to call everything something. I'm skeptical of the specialization that's so pervasive today.

It flies in the face of the current pop church trends to simply say, "We're just a *spiritual* church." I've tried to explain to people that we're the church of utter simplicity, but people seem to have trouble understanding the concept.

For lack of a better term, I call the church of utter simplicity the "Outward-Focused Church." It's a new breed of church that sees beyond church walls and responds to the cry of people to be authentic in serving others. I thought of calling it the generic church, but I didn't think that would convey the spirit of it all that well.

By outward-focused church, I mean the church that is defined simply by what it does rather than by what it says, what it believes, the current programs it offers, or the buildings in which people assemble.

> ## *Distractibility vs. Focus*
>
> **Mr. Maraniss** *(speaking of former president Bill Clinton)*: "Well, he wasn't a bad driver; he was just a totally unconscious driver. He'd be driving around the hills and dales of Arkansas reading a book while he was driving...
>
> **Mr. Williams:** "Oh my gosh."
>
> **Mr. Maraniss:** "...you know, just talking to somebody or gesticulating wildly and scaring the heck out of whoever was in the car with him or whoever was coming the other direction..."[8]

IF YOU'RE NOT OUTWARD-FOCUSED, YOU'RE INWARD-FOCUSED

The temptation for many reading this book will be to respond automatically, "Yeah, we're an outward-focused church. Hurrah for the OF Church!" Caution—don't draw your conclusions so fast. As you read these pages, realize the idea of the OF Church is more of an ideal than a reality that we constantly live in. It's what we aspire to, but, honestly, it's not even where the church I lead lives. The forces of life are powerful and cause all of our churches to be pulled off the outward path on a daily basis.

I coined the term outward-focused church, so I certainly am passionate about making my church, Vineyard Community Church, all about being outwardly focused. In spite of this, I know from vast experience that, because human nature is what it is, programs quickly turn inward in the absence of dogged determination to keep them looking outward.

The great thing about defining what you are about is that you tell people what business you're in. It is dishonest, and way too broad, to simply say, "We are a biblical church." There are hundreds of potential emphases within the vast themes of the Scripture—thus the confusion of the past couple of decades of "bio-driven" churches. Once we stake our claim, once we make a bold and clear statement of the direction we are going and then repeat that statement repeatedly and publicly, we are going to be held accountable.

DON'T BE A SKIP-OCRIT

Friends of mine spent Labor Day weekend of 2000 at the famous Burning Man project. It's an arts festival attended by some of the most unusual, artsy, and high-tech people from around the world. This event, held outside Reno, drew some twenty thousand people, including Kim Corbin, the leader of the worldwide skipping movement. To put it simply, Kim and a few hundred of her followers, are into skipping—really into skipping. The most committed of them skip just about everywhere they go. (However, one of them was observed at Burning Man riding a bicycle. My friends kiddingly accused her of being a "skip"-ocrit.)

When a person makes a bold statement, such as "I am all about skipping; skipping is my life," that person's life becomes very simple and very easy to evaluate. It all comes down to the question, "Are you skipping, or aren't you?" Are you backsliding and just walking, or are you going for it and skipping from place to place? The person who makes such a statement will skip *everywhere* for the *rest of her life*, or she will be seen as a skip-ocrit. (I wonder how she'll handle her wedding march…)

"WE EXIST TO LOVE THIS CITY INTO RELATIONSHIP WITH CHRIST."

In the same way when we make a bold, declarative statement about our reason for existence, people can evaluate how well we're doing it. *"We're here to love our city into relationship with Christ."* Now that can be measured regularly and fairly easily. Are we presenting the simple message of what it takes to follow Christ? Are people making declarations and rededicating their lives to Christ? Are we baptizing people? Are we interacting with our city in creative and regular ways, or are we digging in and talking nonstop about discipleship to the exclusion of outreach?

It took me ten years to come up with this mission statement. I finally nailed it as a result of lots and lots of thinking, mulling, discussing, and discarding dozens—actually hundreds—of ill-fitting ones.

Vision and mission statements are literally inspired by the Holy Spirit.

In the absence of clear direction, churches meander.

"IT'S A JUNGLE OUT THERE;" FINDING OUR WAY BACK

A few months ago, while speaking in southwest Florida, I took a break one Saturday afternoon and went out for an airboat ride with some friends. What an amazing time! With a Chevy engine and an airplane propeller, we hovered just a few inches off the water and zoomed forward at fifty miles per hour. We saw alligators, manatees, water moccasins, rattlers, wild goats, and wild boar. For a bunch of Ohio guys, this was a big-time adventure. And it got bigger when our guide took us in the backwaters of the nearly impenetrable mangrove jungle. When we had gone up and down several miles of jungle canals, he shut the engine off and said, "The Bible says, 'Thou shall not kill.' Out here you don't have to kill someone to get rid of them. Just drop them off for the night."

He later told us that, thirteen years ago, his own son and some friends, all experienced teenage boatmen, had come to the thick mangrove jungle for a day of adventure—and never returned. After weeks of searching, the authorities concluded they had lost their way. There are just that many paths, and the Everglades are just that unforgiving.

The church of today has all the markings of a well-intentioned but inexperienced airboat driver heading off into the Everglades. We may have a general idea of where we should be, but we can't give clear directions about how to get there. Too many distracting possibilities keep us from focusing on our profoundly simple mission—to love others into the kingdom family of Christ. We need a plan.

ENDNOTES

1. Michael Leahy, "Nuns Join Circus, Giving Workers a Place to Run," The Washington Post (May 4, 2000).

2. Craig Van Gelder, *The Essence of the Church* (Grand Rapids, MI: Baker Books, 2000), 24.

3. George Barna, "Pastors Paid Better, But Attendance Unchanged," Barna Research Online, www.barna.org, 1.

4. James Farinet, "Sin Lurks in Faith-Based Plan," The Orlando Sentinel, (28 March, 2001), A17.

5. Richard L. Dunagin, *Beyond These Walls* (Nashville: Abingdon Press, 1999), 29.

6. Toni Morrison, *Paradise* (Westminster, MD: Knopf, 1998).

7. My stories have been given to me over the years. I'm always looking for new descriptions of distracted drivers. If you have a good one, please e-mail it to me at ssjogren@one.net.

8. Juan Williams (Anchor), NPR's *Talk of the Nation*, (23 January, 2001).

9. "Americans Redefine Reckless Driving Habits," Business Wire (14 November, 2000).

ABOUT THE AUTHOR

Steve Sjogren is the launching pastor at Vineyard Community Church, which began in 1983 with a handful of people meeting in various homes around Cincinnati. Today the Vineyard is home to over five thousand regular attendees. The church's mission is to love the people of Cincinnati into relationship with Jesus Christ.

Steve is the author of Conspiracy of Kindness, Servant Warfare*, and* 101 Ways to Reach Your Community*. Steve's heart is for drawing people toward Jesus through simple acts of kindness. He believes that small things done with great love will change the world.*

CHAPTER

2

HOW TO BUILD AN OUTWARD-FOCUSED CHURCH

Evangelism Beyond Church Walls

BY STEVE SJOGREN

In the early days of Vineyard Community Church in Cincinnati, momentum was sluggish, to say the least. The group that I planted the church with believed in "bi-vocational" ministry—in other words, they didn't give much money up front to get things started. My wife and I received a thousand dollars to rent a U-Haul truck and put a down payment on an apartment.

I had a job driving a school bus. At five-thirty one below-zero morning, as I warmed up the bus, I had a talk with God and did a little bit of ventilating. I told God that things hadn't been going all that well. For two years, I had poured a lot of energy into starting that church without seeing much in the way of results.

I sensed that God spoke to me. Since I'm not a morning person, an awareness at that hour that God was speaking to me is especially remarkable. What I heard was something like, "What you're doing is nice. You've gathered some friendly people into a cozy group. You've just got one thing wrong: You're building a 'come and see' church when I want to build a *'go and do'* church."

My first thought was, "If this is God speaking to me, how could he be so rude?" He was saying that I had it all completely backward! I was inviting people into our "cozy" little gathering when he wanted to take those pleasant people and encourage them strongly to go out with the love of Christ.

ROUGH ROW TO HOE

I was adequately depressed at the time to not trust my intuition. As always, I ran my hunch of what the Lord might be saying past my wife, Janie. I was encouraged that she agreed that this might well be the direction the Lord wanted for our group. I began to share the idea with our small groups. "We're going to begin to reach out to the people. Let's become a 'go and do' church instead of a 'come and see' one."

Their first response was excitement. After all, who doesn't like the message, "Let's love humanity." But as the idea sank in and as the practical implications of what this would look like began to trickle down, a percentage of the group began to turn against the idea.

"We're not ready to do this." "I don't think we're healed enough to do this yet." "We're not trained to do this." (How much training does it take to show people kindness by washing cars for free?). At first I couldn't believe my ears as excuses for not getting out into the community poured in.

The words of Charles Schulz (a la his *Peanuts* character Linus) came back to me, "I love mankind; it's people I can't stand."

The idea of doing evangelism is a frightening notion for most Christians. It conjures up images of highly stylistic approaches to sharing the gospel message that just don't seem natural. But what if the goal wasn't to do what has always been done? What if the goal was simply to be effective? What if the goal wasn't to focus on one highly gifted leader to do all the work but simply to find approaches that allow the average follower of Christ to do simple works of outreach?

My story is finding these approaches. That's been my heartbeat for fifteen years of experimenting as a leader in outreach and church planting.

Both the "come and see" and the "go and do" message can be found in Scripture. The Samaritan woman at the well said, "*Come, see* a man who told me everything I ever did" (John 4:29, emphasis added). "Go and do" is also found in the Bible, and far more frequently than the "come and see" message. Not only is the message clearly laid out in the five Great Commission texts that Jesus gave (Matthew 28; Mark 16; Luke 24; John 20; Acts 1), but from Genesis through the New Testament, the Bible story becomes more and more "go and do."

SURVIVAL BY OUTWARDNESS

Today's church has become so irrelevant that it is virtually invisible to the culture around it. Author Alan J. Roxburgh calls this liminality. Instead of mourning the loss of our influence during this time of irrelevancy, we ought to see the amazing opportunities at hand. But those opportunities won't come in the same way they have presented themselves in the past, nor will they come in traditional packaging.

"Liminality requires listening again to those voices emanating from below or outside the perceived mainstream."[1] What are those voices saying that we need to be listening to? They are saying four key words: *definition, stimulation, speculation* and *experimentation*.

DEFINITION

Give Away What You Don't Have

In the first few years of our church plant in Cincinnati, we didn't pretend to have it all together. We knew we could not fulfill the typical American churchgoer's expectation of a full-service church. For example, we didn't have a youth group, and Sunday school was often more about baby-sitting than spiritual training. So we focused on the few things we could do well. We wanted worship that would draw people into God's presence. We sought to have messages that were practical, simple, and biblical. Having open hearts to welcome whomever came through the doors and finding ways to serve our way into the hearts of the people in our community became a priority.

In those early years, these concepts were in such "seed" form that we often directed the people we met in the community to other churches. We'd say, "You don't want to come to our church, at least, not yet. It really lacks quality at this point. Come in a couple of years. We'll have our act more together then."

When people protested, saying, "But we really would like to check out what you are doing," we'd say, "No, you ought to visit the Baptist church down the street or the really good Assembly of God church across town. They have a lot to offer."

In a sense we were inviting people to an experience with God that we couldn't offer yet. But that didn't stop us from inviting them to the experience.

We grew to a few hundred people and found a building we wanted to purchase. At the same time, a local mega-mall offered us an opportunity to get involved in an outreach to the community by wrapping gifts between Thanksgiving and Christmas. This outreach was a huge investment of time, energy, and money for our small church. In fact, the amount of money we needed for the outreach was about half of what we needed for a down payment on a new facility. Typical human reasoning would have dictated that we scale back, play it safe, call off the outreach, and save our money for the building.

However, God usually presents opportunities for outreach when we can least afford them, at least on paper. So we jumped in with both feet and chose not to compromise outreach even for a "good" cause. We challenged our people to "pray, serve, and give." Not only did we serve over ten thousand people with our gift-wrap outreach, we also met our building down-payment goal and had our first celebration service on Super Bowl Sunday!

Do You Speak "Dechurched"?

Church futurist George Barna writes that we're no longer talking simply about the "unchurched" when we refer to those who are outside Christ and beyond the grasp of an organized approach to following Christ. Barna states that we have a more challenging group to communicate with—the "dechurched," who have concluded that the entire notion of organized religion, including following Christ and attending church, is a complete waste of time.[2] From my experience in talking to these folks, the dechurched think churches exist for three reasons: to raise money, to parent people, and to promote themselves.

For the past fifteen years, I have been doing "servant evangelism," which means totally free acts of generosity to demonstrate to people the love of Christ. My friends and I will wash cars for free, for example. I've found that, when we don't promote our own church but the church as a whole, it takes people back.

A couple of years ago, we realized that our free outreaches had been so effective that too much attention had been focused on our church in Cincinnati. We began to do outreaches in the names of other churches to promote them! Now when we go out to do an outreach, more often than not we do an act of kindness or serve people then hand them a card with the name of another church in town and a map to that church's location.

God has given us great joy and satisfaction in giving ourselves away. Deep down we're givers. When we determine to be who we are and walk that path out, we become the most effective we can possibly be. We are redefining church to the community.

Big Idea: Be Yourself

I was honored to be a seminar presenter at Billy Graham's Amsterdam 2000 event. The event was spectacular. More than eleven thousand people from all over the world gathered simply to focus on

Do Unto Others

As newspaper advice columnists such as Ann Landers who have been at their trade for decades approach the twilight of their careers, younger advice-givers are coming forward. One of the rising syndicated stars is Carolyn Hax. Not only does she write for numerous newspapers, but she also contributes to Self Magazine and has written an advice-giving book. Her advice about giving great advice is simple. "All I do is rewrite the golden rule in three answers per column, twice a week, fifty-two weeks a year," Hax said.[3]

the topic of evangelism. It was a thrill to rub elbows with people who have given themselves heart and soul to the task of reaching the world with the gospel of Christ.

On the other hand, it was odd. I saw people from about every culture in the world; you name it, they were there. It was beautiful to see them be themselves in Christ when they weren't "on" as evangelists. But when it was time for them to switch on and become evangelists, some of them became different people. They seemed a lot like Texans instead of being Zambians, Norwegians, or Mexicans. When they went into evangelist mode, they acted differently, they walked differently, they definitely talked differently—they just weren't the same people.

Our greatest asset in connecting with the dechurched is authenticity. People see through our attempts at playing a role. Yet, even if we're uncomfortable doing it, we think we should play the part. How much more could the Spirit use us if we determined to be nothing more or less than ourselves? What if we were just ourselves in our attempts at outreach? What you do speaks louder than words.

Do As He Does, Not As He Says

When I was growing up, my most interesting uncle was a retired sailor. My mom used to say he cussed "like a sailor." I know that comparison is not very PC (politically correct), but I guess in that day it was typical for career sailors to cuss quite a bit. Uncle Joe couldn't string two sentences together without throwing in a colorful cuss-word or two. Later in life, his hard living caught up with him. He came down with larynx cancer and had to speak with a special vibrator that made him sound like a robot.

Even though he had gone through all the cancer-related hardship and had come to faith in Christ at his Baptist church in Missouri, he still cussed "like a sailor" and sounded like a robot. Yet this man was one of the kindest, most generous, and most considerate people I've met. When we went out to eat, he always insisted on paying for everyone. When he came to visit, he showered me with gifts, even though he was not a particularly wealthy man. To this day, he stands out as one of the people I've been blessed to meet. When I was a child, my dad gave me instructions about Uncle Joe before each visit. He explained, "Normally you will hear people say, 'Do as he says, but not as he does,' because some people are hypocrites. But in Joe's case—he's a great guy; one of the best. Think the opposite: 'Do as he does, just don't say as he says.' "

We might be offended by the speech of an ill-fitting old man who doesn't conform—and miss a lifestyle that's sterling. The church today is the opposite of Uncle Joe. It's a place with much fine talk—spiritually PC language—that's technically correct but wrong in heart and empty of practical application. The right things might be said, but so precious little is acted upon. What's worse: cussing or much talk with no action behind it? Our culture no longer hears the church talk, but people sure are watching closely what we do.

STIMULATION

Build an Atmosphere

In order for outreach to succeed, we must create atmospheres that allow faith to dwell. By *atmosphere*, I mean a setting where it feels normal to give away ourselves, our goods, and our energy with great generosity.

Atmosphere—it's what is felt before anything specific is experienced.

As an author, I do a lot of radio interviews to discuss my recently published books. Most of these interviews include live phone calls from listeners. I usually talk about the power of simple acts of kindness to change hearts,[4] and the most common questions from the callers are, "Why do you do this? It's to build your church, right? Is it just pretty clever advertising, or what?"

I always respond, "We love, serve, and care for others because that is normal behavior for people who are filled with God's Spirit. We are Christians. Christ was the ultimate servant. We can't help but serve because the Spirit of the Servant has filled our hearts. When we serve, we are just being who we naturally are." As we live out that natural supernaturalness, we are creating a larger-than-life atmosphere that brings change to the world.

A Contagious Atmosphere

An atmosphere touches all who come near it. When we build an atmosphere, we extend our influence enormously. In other words, the sum of our influence is greater than the parts of our physical presence.

A program will touch people one to one, a few people here and there. An atmosphere is something that's almost out of control, but in the very best sense of the concept.

Heartland Community Church in Lawrence, Kansas, sponsored a Gasoline Buy Down outreach to the city. For two hours, church members sold gas for about fifty cents a gallon less than the normal price. They pumped the gasoline, checked the oil, and gave out soft drinks to customers. That day they did more than just do a program for outreach. They created something that was larger than life. They built an atmosphere. Consider the summarized result Pastor Paul Gray e-mailed me after the outreach. The atmosphere comes across even in the e-mail.

Here's the results:

23 Heartland members served the people of Lawrence

3,140 gallons of gasoline were pumped

$1,413 was the savings to the public (HCC paid $1,000 and
the station unexpectedly covered $413!)

785 people came in

314 cars got gas

$4.50 was the average benefit per car

240 cans of pop were given out

200+ cups of coffee were given out

100+ balloons were given away (compliments of the
station)

250+ windows were washed

4 newspapers ran articles

2 TV stations featured stories

1 radio station did a 30-minute interview

Thousands of people in Lawrence heard about the event!

There was tremendous excitement at Heartland!

Risking it all for Him,

Paul Gray

Now that's an atmosphere! At the end of the day, nearly the entire university town of Lawrence had either heard or read or was told about the gasoline buy down. The gospel was being gossiped about in an out-of-control way.

THE TOILET CHURCH—A HEALING PLACE

One of the most electric, memorable atmospheres I've spoken in was also one of the most ironic settings. I receive invitations to speak at all sorts of churches, including one in Neza, Mexico (a suburb of Mexico City). This two-year-old church is made up of several hundred people who are mostly people in process. Many are coming out of drug addictions or lives of prostitution. The majority of attendees make their living picking through trash in the nearby dumps.

The church meets in a converted public restroom. In Mexico City, one has to pay to use the facilities. This church used to be such a place. In fact, there are still holes in the floor where the commodes once sat. The roof of the facility is a tent made of discarded vinyl road signs that have been sewn together. One sign promises better gas mileage with the use of Mobil oil; another says something in Spanish about a new brand of chocolate.

The worship at this church is phenomenal. Though I couldn't understand the language, I found the experience downright healing, from the sense of God's Spirit that was present to the conga line dancing.

Auto Atmospheres

Bumper stickers create some great atmospheres for other drivers. Check out these recently chosen "Best of" bumper stickers.

Coffee. Now!

Too bad ignorance isn't painful.

Stop Global Whining

Give Blood—Play Hockey

My Gun Is Safer Than Ted Kennedy's Car

Nude Driver—Don't Look

HWJD—How Would Jesus Drive?

At Least I'm Not Driving an Aztek!

The Voices Told Me to Stay Home and Clean the Guns Today

I'm Not Tailgating, I'm Drafting

So Many Cats, So Few Recipes!

Sometimes I Wake Up Grouchy. Sometimes I Just Let Her Sleep!

COLMA, CALIFORNIA

Some atmospheres aren't quite as positive or life-giving. A friend of mine actually lives in one such place: Colma, California. If it wasn't for the cheap real estate, he'd live elsewhere. Colma, a suburb about two miles south of San Francisco, sprang up during the past few decades as land values grew in the city. Over the years, even cemetery plots became too expensive to maintain in the city on the bay, so cemeteries all around the San Francisco area started a relocation plan. In San Francisco, what were once cemetery sites are now condos and high rises.

And Colma? It's home to over 1.5 million inhabitants—and all but one thousand are underground. The luminaries buried there include Wyatt Earp, and Tina Turner's dog, which is rumored to be wrapped in a mink stole. The motto of its few and proud living souls: *"It's great to be alive in Colma!"* [5]

The church often looks a lot like Colma, California. British author Os Guinness argues that the church is *"privately engaging, socially irrelevant."* [6] We have lots of history, and we're big on promises, but we're not much when it comes to atmosphere or life in the present. We don't want our churches to be considered the place where the dead are sent, while the real living goes on elsewhere.

SPECULATION

Build First—Details Later

Not long ago, Cincinnati was in the national news because of racial tensions following the shooting of an unarmed young African-American man who was wanted for what amounted to a few traffic violations. The city erupted into all-out riots. Weeklong curfews followed in this normally conservative river city.

A good friend of mine is the pastor of the family of the young man who was killed. As the heavily covered funeral service was quickly put together, my friend and I brainstormed about outreach to the highly charged atmosphere. In a crowd with several thousand protesters carrying signs with expletives directed at the police, white people, and city officials, we went to work as ad hoc caterers. We served three thousand chicken-sandwich lunches with drinks. That evening we made it on CNN's national news coverage of the event with the lead—"Church answers racially charged event with the power of kindness."

Behind the news story was another story about stepping out and taking a risk. We had tried for several days to get the OK from the city to go ahead with the outreach at the funeral. Because of the rioting, communication was difficult. It came down to the wire the day before the event. We had to order food for three thousand by four o'clock Friday afternoon, but the chief of police wasn't able to get back to us until later that night. We went for it on faith and said to ourselves, "If nothing else, we'll feed people as they drive away from the funeral." At eight o'clock that night, we received a call giving us permission, an escort, and a great location for the giveaway.

Lesson: Sometimes you just have to jump before all of the answers come in. God will take care of the details.

I like the wisdom of Pastor Doug Roe: "Jump and the net will appear" (see Chapter 6). Most churches can't handle that sort of thinking. Conventional thinking in virtually all congregations I'm familiar with is, "Think long and hard, gather all the statistics and studies available, get some consultants involved, vote multiple times on the proposal, and then, if there is a windfall in the budget, consider stepping in—but never, ever actually *jump.*" Finally, after two to three years of talking and stammering about the issue, the church is ready to take a bit of action.

The Bible gives repeated warnings about the foolishness of deciding matters too quickly. For example, Proverbs 18:13b says, "Yes, how stupid!—to decide before knowing the facts!" and Proverbs 22:3 tells us, "A prudent man foresees the difficulties ahead and prepares for them; the simpleton goes blindly on and suffers the consequences" (The Living Bible). The Bible also gives us the other side of the coin. In Ecclesiastes 11:4, we find, "If you wait for perfect conditions, you will never get anything done" (NLT).

Anyone who has been in the church long enough to attend a committee meeting knows what it's like to err on the side of caution. Our histories show that we've been led by drill sergeants with Alzheimer's who are stuck on the command "Ready, Aim...Ready, Aim...Ready, Aim..." It would almost be therapeutic for many congregations, elder boards, and pastoral teams to make a few decisions based on action instead of following the age-old, neurotic ways of caution. Let's do some "Ready, FIRE, Aim" actions.

Just Say "So" and "Mo" (Sodalities and Modalities)

The "Ready-Aim" approach is a typical pattern for what is called a "modality" orientation. Missiologist Ralph Winter has explained that there are two approaches to getting ministry done in the church—modality and the sodality.

Modalities are the status quo, the experts, the way we've always done things. Sodalities are the opposite. They are the amateurs; they are experimental and decentralized.

We need both of these approaches to doing ministry to succeed. We must have the "regular" approach, and then we need to be open to the "experimental" way of doing things, as well.

When it comes to outward-focused approaches, however, it's the sodality approach that needs to be given leeway. Being too careful and worrying too much about risks will kill our outreach. The strength of the modality is its ability to ask good questions and keep things legal, moral, and ethical. But the modalic approach to ministry gets easily stuck on "Ready, Aim…Ready, Aim…" in the starting gates. The sodalic approach is what's needed to get new ministry off the ground so that risks can be taken. A "Ready, FIRE!, Aim" approach can be good for an organization that's stuck.

> *"We don't actually do what we propose—we just propose it."*
>
> —from UPS TV commercial

We need both the experts and the amateurs for the work of the kingdom to be accomplished through the church. Most of the time in the local church, we've heard too much from the experts and not enough from the amateurs.

EXPERIMENTATION

Getting Past the Theoretical to Doing Something

A show that has aired to a vast viewing audience on MTV is called simply *Jacka*** (you get the idea). In case you haven't seen it, it offers half-hour segments filled with physical dares to do absolutely outlandish stunts that range between gross, unsafe (being slapped across the face baseball-bat fashion with a twenty-pound salmon), and nearly suicidal (being shot at point-blank range with a .38 caliber pistol while wearing a Kevlar vest "just to see if it hurt").

In a day when millions long to be participants and not mere observers, this show has gotten phenomenal ratings by all accounts. The show's star, Johnny Knoxville, has landed three movies at $1 million per gig.[7]

Apologies for offending the sensibilities of any reader who is put off by the name of this show, but that's really its name, and it really is part of the mainstream pop culture today.

The question this show's popularity raises is, why is it such a phenomena? Is it because of the odd stunts? the possibility of someone getting hurt? the raw creativity in each episode?

Yes, perhaps a bit of all of these is right. I think it goes deeper, however. We are living in a time when people are more than ever wanting to do more than theorize. This generation could well have as its motto, "To *do* so is better than to *say* so!"

In a strange way, Johnny Knoxville has gained the respect of millions of viewers because he puts his money where his mouth is. He puts himself in the line of fire.

Very much like the star of *The Crocodile Hunter* on cable TV's Animal Planet, he isn't one who writes books about adventure. He actually has several adventures in each episode and invites us to go along with him for the ride. And we respect him for what he is doing.

In past generations, it was enough to know about a topic to qualify as an "expert." Now our culture demands that we actually do what we talk about.

I am writing a book on church planting. It's a specialized topic; I suspect that not many people out there have a desire to read about church planting or who are the people planting churches. As I did market research about the existing church planting books, I was surprised to discover something interesting about almost all church planting books. With very few exceptions, they have been written by seminary professors who have never actually planted a church. The unique angle of this new book is that it's written by a guy who has actually planted quite a few churches;

it's a book about church planting written by someone who's actually planted churches. Go figure. That shouldn't be newsworthy, but unfortunately it is. Now that's not to say these other authors aren't smart guys. They are very nice guys—some of them are friends of mine, but they are writing about topics they haven't actually experienced. The church seems to be the last place in our society that is willing to listen to the theoreticians who lack experience.

Let's have some adventures in doing the outward-focused church. Let's not just think about it—let's dive in headfirst and begin to change the face of the church and the way the dechurched think about following Christ.

ENDNOTES

1. Alan J. Roxburgh, *The Missionary Congregation, Leadership, and Liminality* (Harrisburg, PA: Trinity Press International, 1997), 46-47.

2. George Barna, *Rechurching the Unchurched*, (Ventura, CA: Issachar Resources, 2000).

3. Eric R. Danton, "Carolyn Hax Didn't Plan Career in Advice Business," Star Tribune, Minneapolis, MN, (March 31, 2001), 5E.

4. This message is covered in detail in my books *Conspiracy of Kindness* (Vine Books, 1993) and *101 Ways to Reach Your Community* (NavPress, 2001). Both are available by dialing 888.KINDNESS

5. Lisa Taggart, "Home of the Grave," Sunset Magazine, (October 1, 2000) 44.

6. Michael Obel, "Anglican Probes Christianity's Declining Influence," United Press International, (June 29, 1984).

7. Erik Hedegaard, "The King of Pain—Jackass," Rolling Stone (February 1, 2001), 40-44; 64.c

CHAPTER 3

RUINING YOUR MINISTRY FOR GOOD

Seeing the "Missed" Beyond Church Walls

BY
BRIAN D.
McLAREN

I t was Sunday. I had the day off because another of our pastors preached. It was a good day for me. I had preached about eighteen weeks straight, and it was good to be just a member of the congregation—to listen, to pray, to sing, to take communion, to hang out with people after the first service.

Without any public responsibilities (no preaching, welcome, benediction, or communion), I was pretty relaxed, so I wandered around the church during the second service. I gave little kids high fives in the hallways, hugged people I haven't hugged for a long time, stuck my head in the Sunday School classes and gave a smile and wink to each teacher, and listened without hurry to the people who wanted to talk to me. Sad to say, it's been awhile since I did these things.

A GOOD DAY

A woman standing at the auditorium doors handing out bulletins was familiar, but I had never really talked to her. Today I did.

"My boyfriend and I have been coming for about a year now," she said. "This experience has changed our lives." After the service, I noticed that she and her boyfriend cleaned up after coffee and donuts—a sure sign that they really belong now! I learned that he was once a drummer in a nationally known rock band. After a fast and furious stint with designer drugs and alcohol, he left music, lost everything, and got into recovery. Coming to church was part of his growth in his recovery process. Here, he and his girlfriend discovered that the higher power who was helping restore them to sanity was in fact the God and Father of Jesus Christ.

That was this morning. Yesterday, I was in a planning meeting all day with a group that's helping us design and lead a new service. Looking around the room, I saw fourteen people. That fellow there—the one who's about thirty—I remember him coming to church about seven years ago. He wasn't a Christian then, but now he's leading this group. In the back of the room sits a middle-aged couple. The husband and wife were both alienated churchgoers who had returned to church, and to faith, about five years ago, after many years away. Now they're becoming leaders too. The gal in the front row, who is just twenty and a little insecure about being there, wasn't a Christian five months ago and is just beginning to call herself one now. Two women sit together in the fourth row; one isn't a Christian yet but is progressing toward Christ fast, and her friend is about two steps ahead of her. An intellectual, a college professor, she was devoted to New Age religion for many years and is surprised to find herself praying and growing in a Christian church. She just volunteered to head up one of the ministry teams for this new service.

Why am I telling you this? Because today I realized how fortunate I am. I am in a church that has turned inside out (and thus right side up). I am privileged to be part of an outward-focused church—a church that is welcoming new people and seeing some of them become followers of Jesus.

PROBLEMS A-PLENTY

Sure, we have our problems—plenty of them. I won't tell you about all the sexual messes, personal problems, financial catastrophes, relapses, doubts, odd beliefs, and misunderstandings these people bring with them. We're dealing with what they bring but often with less success than more. I won't tell you about the bad behavior from many of our Christians that has at times almost driven some of these spiritual seekers away. Nor will I go into the ways the questions posed by our spiritual seekers have upset my own faith at times because my old answers seemed flimsy and frail against the strength of their new questions.

I won't go into all that because these problems are the problems I prefer having, so I feel fortunate, blessed, to have them. I think many pastors would gladly trade us their problems: petty squabbling about trivial-pursuit doctrines or religious practices; people whining, "my needs aren't being met; you're not feeding me"; and pressure to keep up with the latest spiritual fads. You're thinking, "I'd like to become outward-focused, too, and trade for that set of problems!"

Now if you're expecting a "here's how we became outward-focused, and you can, too, in just five easy steps, each beginning with the letter S"—well, sorry. It doesn't work that way. The church-growth seminars of the late '80s and early '90s taught us all something: Learning new techniques, adapting new programs, or imitating new models just doesn't produce. What needs to change is deeper than techniques or programs. It's not just our churches that need to change; it's us.

BAD NEWS

But here's the bad news: When you start to change, you will ruin your ministry as it now is. Did you read that previous sentence? Because I meant it. Your ministry (as it is) will be ruined if you change in the ways we are considering in this book. True, your ministry will be ruined for a good cause, and that good cause will, in fact, become your new ministry. But don't underestimate the cost of seeing ministry as you know it ruined for good.

In my first book, I said that we have to face the fact that having "seeker-sensitive services" counts for little if we don't have "seeker-sensitive Christians." In other words, if our Christians don't love (and like) non-Christians, then all our talk about change and renewal won't mean beans. But if our Christians *do* love and like non-Christians, then watch out. Ministry as we know it is ruined—for good (in both senses of the phrase).

In the years since writing my first book, I've realized more and more that we won't become seeker-sensitive

Christians until we take a long and hard look at our theology. I think our inward-focused churches are, ultimately, an accurate reflection of our deepest theology. In short, we have inward-focused churches because we have an inward-focused theology. You can talk about changing your "methods" all you want, but face it, as soon as you start talking about changing your theology, your ministry is ruined. For good!

So maybe you should just forget about this whole outward-focused thing. It's too costly. Too risky. You have too much to lose. Maybe there's something good on TV.

A TRIP TO THE DOCTOR

If you're still reading, I'll assume you're crazy enough to actually consider ruining your ministry for good. And, if that's the case, you need your head examined. So let me fill the role of doctor for you and start the examination.

If you go to a doctor, he or she generally asks, "How have you been feeling?" and "Where does it hurt?"

The doctor is likely to pull out a little rubber hammer or shine a bright light in your eyes to see how you react. Based on your responses and reactions to the intrusions (many of which are uncomfortable), the doctor can help you see what's wrong with you and figure out what to do about it.

So, here are my two diagnostic questions. Just think about them and maybe talk about them with some of the leaders of your church.

1. Do you really believe God loves the world?

The fact is, your theology may be reinterpreting the gospel this way: "For God hated the world so much that he sent his only Son, so that whoever believes in him could be removed from the world, so he can save the believers and go ahead and damn the world, which he really hates…For God sent his Son into the world to condemn the world and to save the church."

Now, if the hair on the back of your neck is rising and you're ready to pull out a rather mean name to call me ("universalist" or "liberal," for example), please resist that urge. Instead of trying to diagnose me, examine your own theology for a few minutes. We can deal with my problems some other time; right now, I'm the doctor, and we're talking about you. I'll ask again: Do you really believe that God loves the world?

2. Do you believe the church exists for the benefit of the world or that the world exists for the benefit of the church?

The fact is, according to the theology many of us hold, the church is like a city and the world is like a mountain that is being strip mined and logged to build the city. We don't really care about the mountain; it's only there for our benefit. "To hell with the world—and to heaven with the church" could well be our motto. Is it your motto?

OK, now for the little rubber hammer and the bright light—please get ready for a whack on your "funny bone," which won't feel very funny, and for a beam shining in your pupil, which may make you cry. Ready?

If you don't really believe that God loves the world (the whole thing—the Christians, the Jews, the Moslems, the Buddhists, the trees, the plankton, the ozone layer, the topsoil, the swamps, the sea turtles, the frogs, the orangutans—the whole thing) and if you believe the world exists as a mine for the benefit of the church, then maybe it's better that you stay inward focused! Maybe it's best that you win no more converts. Maybe you should just keep singing praise songs and having all-night prayer meetings and being busy with Bible studies and circling the wagons and isolating from non-Christians. Maybe it's best that you get mad and put this book down and remained confirmed in your ways.

Why? Because if your theology doesn't affirm that God loves the world, then every new person you bring in will, in turn, make the world a worse place, a more hated place, and doing so will, in fact, work against the progress of the gospel and the kingdom of God. (If I were preaching, I'd repeat that sentence verbatim, maybe twice. So maybe you should go back and read it again.) If you have a "God-hates-the-world" theology, your new follower may become a good charismatic, or evangelical, or fundamentalist, or whatever—but the follower will be other than, and less than, a disciple of Jesus Christ. You will be making more religious people, perhaps, but maybe…maybe…they will be more like inward-focused Pharisees than outward-focused disciples.

(I'm sorry. The preceding paragraphs probably seem harsh and exaggerated. Remember, they were supposed to be like hammer taps to test your reflex reactions. I wasn't trying to hurt you or be rude; I'm just trying to reach a good diagnosis that will help you ruin your ministry for a good cause.)

UNSETTLING CONCLUSIONS

This kind of questioning and hammering is probably unsettling. It should be. If there's any legitimacy at all to what I'm saying, we need to be unsettled. Remember, we're talking about ruining your ministry (for good), not saving it or improving it or renewing it.

I'll tell you who started unsettling me. He was a theologian, already well into his eighties. A retired missionary, he had left England, spent forty years in India, and then returned to England. His time away gave him a fresh perspective on his native country and the western civilization of which it is part. His forty years engaging in evangelism in another culture, in the midst of people of another religion, made him reexamine not only his native culture but also his native culture's interpretation of the Bible, the gospel, and the church.

His name was Lesslie Newbigin. I never met him, but I have read and re-read many of his books. I didn't read them because they made me feel good, but because they kept hitting me like a doctor's rubber hammer or bright beam, causing me to twitch and jump, making my eyes water—and challenging me to think new thoughts. Lesslie Newbigin is partly responsible for ruining my ministry for good.

The self-diagnosis I reached was this: my theology sincerely attempted to be biblical, but it had become so enmeshed with modernity, American consumerism, modern western rationalism, and a host of other things, that it somehow was out of synch with Jesus Christ. Through Newbigin's writings, I realized I was a Christian who needed to be reached for Christ. My ministry as it was needed to be ruined for good.

To put it more sharply (though perhaps less poignantly), I believed in Christ and wanted to follow Christ; but my view of the world, my unbelieving neighbors, and my mission in the world seemed different from the view of Jesus Christ. That needed to change.

ELECT ELITE OR SELECT SERVANTS?

My theology—and maybe yours is like mine was—told

me that God loved me and wanted to bless me eternally. I had been "elected," or chosen, for privilege. The "them" of the world were a threat to me; they wanted to draw me away from God, and they mocked my faith or threatened to make me doubt it. I had a lot to lose, so naturally, I feared them. My encounters with them (which I had many reasons to avoid altogether) always tended to be of an aggressive nature: I wanted to change them before they polluted me. Enjoy them? Laugh with them? Eat with them? Encourage them? No! It was my job to scare the hell out of them, if I could, so they'd want to become like me.

Newbigin proposed a different view. His theology said that God loved the world (really! loved…the world!). It said that one of the ways God wanted to bless the world was by first blessing me, then connecting me with a community of other blessed people, and then sending us to be a blessing to others—all others. In his understanding, I had been "elected," or chosen, for responsibility, service, mission, even suffering…not privilege. All of this was for the benefit of the world, not merely for my personal advantage or the aggrandizement of the church. My neighbors were not a threat; they were the people to whom I had been sent as an agent of Jesus Christ, as a carrier of his spirit and grace. If they believed, they were signing on to be agents of Christ too. If they didn't, nothing changed. I was still chosen to be an agent of Christ toward them.

That simple concept has worked like a computer virus—a good virus—over these last several years. It has rearranged my data, uncorrupted my files, defragmented my hard drive, and scanned my disks for non-gospel error messages. It ruined ministry as I knew it for good.

Maybe that's why I felt so good today as I talked to that woman by the door of the auditorium and reflected on yesterday's planning meeting with that motley crew of saints/sinners/seekers. I felt that I had been changed and that my conversion was spreading to others. I felt that somehow my faith, my theology, had been turned inside out. A message of personal advantage ("how to get my butt into heaven") had become a message of global service ("how to join God in his love for the world"). Somehow, that approach feels more in synch with Jesus Christ. I guess I'm as excited about my faith turning inside out as I am about my church turning inside out.

FIVE WAYS WE WERE RUINED

Again, this change process in my life and in our church hasn't been neat, nor has it been easy. It has caused some people to leave, including good friends and people I really felt we needed. But at the end of the day, I would never reverse the revolution. Nor would I stop it now, because I know we're not done yet. We still have a lot to learn and a long way to go. If you embark, I believe you'll feel the same way. Let me conclude by briefly summarizing a few of the many ways we were ruined for good.

1. *Our language was ruined.* Obviously, we couldn't just throw around our insider vocabulary any more, with talk about sanctification, conviction, raising up leaders and lifting up prayer requests, and ministering to the body. We started becoming sensitive to how these terms came across to our friends (Ministering to *the body?* What, do you do massage therapy here or something?), these folks whom we loved and to whom these words sounded bizarre and confusing. We had to convey the meanings in new ways, and that was hard for us. We had to incarnate those meanings in stories (as Jesus did), or explain them in terms of metaphors (the way Jesus did). In the process, we often realized that, although we had used these words for years, when it came to really explaining them, we had little idea what they really meant! This realization was humbling and embarrassing and frustrating for us, and we didn't like it.

Even more frustrating: we used to call people outside the church names—*unsaved, lost, secular,* and *non-Christians,* for example. These labels were very convenient for us, and they made us feel better about ourselves, as if we had a superior status in the world. Perhaps there was some technical validity to each of these labels, but after we started really loving our neighbors outside the church, the technical validity didn't matter. Those terms were ruined for us because we realized the labels reinforced an unaccept-able sense of superiority in us and a corresponding sense of isolation and rejection in our neighbors. Life was much sim-pler when everyone fit into a neat category: in-group or out-group, found or lost, saved or damned. But as Peter learned during his visit to Caesarea that he should never call any person "impure or unclean" (Acts 10:28), we learned that "in-grouping" and "out-grouping" are ruined for us for good. ("Well, then," you might be asking, "what do you call...those people?" You'll never believe it, but it turns out that they have *names,* just as we do!)

2. *Our fellowship was ruined.* You see, it used to be that "we" were all alike. We all knew the same songs, liked the same political candidates, held the same political opinions, and had similar stores of Bible knowledge. So we all got the same jokes (like the one about the smallest man in the Bible, the first motorcycle rider in the Bible, or...). We all knew what was acceptable to wear, to say ("crap" and "shoot" and "darn" were OK, but other parallel words weren't), to drink (root beer, yes; real beer…?).

But when our new friends came in, everything got messy. Yes, there were new rewards, new challenges, new thrills, and many wonderful benefits. In fact, the word *fellowship* took on a whole new dimension and depth. Nevertheless, fellowship as we knew it was ruined.

3. My preaching was ruined. I used to begin every sermon with the same words: "Please open your Bibles to…" and a book, chapter, and verse reference would follow. Now, I can't start my sermons that way for a number of reasons. First, the people don't have Bibles. Increasingly, if you ask them to study something on their own, they'll look it up online. If they have a hard copy at all, it's a page printed from the online Bible. Second, even if they do have Bibles, they're not "normal" like us. They don't know the books of the Bible, so they can't look things up fast. They never learned those Sunday school songs that help you find things. Third, even if they could find the passage, they might not understand what I said. Inherent in my former quoting of the Bible was a whole set of assumptions about the Bible's historical authenticity, spiritual authority, and interpretive method. These new friends don't share these assumptions. I can't take them for granted. Instead of assuming the Bible's authority and relevance and usefulness, and instead of arguing for them, I have to demonstrate them every week.

Finally, when your audience doesn't assume the Bible's authority and interpretive grid, you can't preach deductively ("The Bible says X, so therefore you must do Y and Z"). You can't dissect verses and give all kinds of cool alliterated outlines (The 4 Ps of Romans 5, The 6 Cs of Philippians 3) and impress your friends while proving points by referring to the Greek. Instead, you have to be interesting...I mean, interesting to anybody, not just people who already have a thirst for Bible esoterica. You have to tell stories and work with language and imagine how a conversation would flow and unfold and take turns and switchbacks and leaps and reversals. True, when you do that, you end up preaching more in the manner of Jesus. But that's not what I was used to. Preaching as I knew it was ruined for good.

4. *Our evangelism was ruined.* It was so simple before. I didn't realize that nearly everything I knew about evangelism was conditioned by nineteenth century revivalism and twentieth century salesmanship. I thought all those methods and diagrams and outlines were divinely inspired. Surely Jesus drew the Bridge diagram in the dust that day when the woman caught in adultery was about to be stoned, and surely Paul used the four spiritual laws when speaking on Mars Hill, even though it's not exactly recorded that way. Everybody knew that you became a Christian by saying "the sinner's prayer," even though there really aren't any such prayers mandated by or even exemplified in Scripture. Everybody knew that salvation occurred at a certain definable moment, so that at youth rallies, when they sing "It was on a Monday...Somebody touched me...must have been the hand of the Lord!"—you would know when to stand up.

But then we got outward focused. New people started coming to our church, people who refused to "get saved" at a clearly definable point as they're supposed to. Maybe they could sing, "It was in the '90s...Somebody touched me," but it didn't seem to get much more specific than that! Evangelism was ruined! They would ask the really profound theological questions that only seminarians are supposed to grapple with…but they would ask these questions before they were even committed Christians. They would want to go on mission trips and play in the worship band and give large sums of money…when they hadn't even "said the sinner's prayer" yet! Yet it was clear that they were becoming genuine followers of Christ—just not in the ways we were used to. Evangelism was ruined for us, for good.

5. *Our reputation was ruined.* When we started changing, rethinking, struggling, questioning, and wrestling with all these new issues—when we found out that becoming outward-focused meant that we were becoming a different kind of Christian than we used to be—some of our fellow Christians started wondering about us. They heard that we had homosexuals attending our services, as well as people who were living together but not yet married and people (leaders even!) who believed in evolution, and they had no choice but to wonder about us. Obviously, we were lowering our standards. We must be dumbing down, watering down, and loosening up. They heard that we started quoting Catholics, including Henri Nouwen, Thomas Merton, and St. John of the Cross, and it was pretty clear to them that we weren't the same old conservative Protestant evangelicals we used to be. We seemed to still love the Lord, but…

And they were right. I mean, they were wrong when they accused us of dumbing down, watering down, and loosening up. But they were right that we were changing. Make no mistake: seeing beyond your walls is not just a nice program you add to your existing list of programs so that everything just goes on as before, except maybe even a little bigger and better. No—any more than marriage is just adding another person to your income tax return, with no other substantive changes to your life! Becoming outward-focused will ruin your ministry for good. In both senses of the phrase.

But most days, especially today, I'm glad we're on this journey. I would never be "un-ruined." This ruination is for good.

ABOUT THE AUTHOR

Brian McLaren is the founding pastor of Cedar Ridge Community Church, an innovative church in the Baltimore-Washington region. About 55 percent of the church's attenders were previously unchurched. Brian has been active in networking church planters and pastors since the mid '80s and has assisted in the development of several new churches. He is a frequent guest lecturer at national and international seminaries and conferences.

McLaren has written four books on postmodern ministry, apologetics, and evangelism: The Church on the Other Side: Doing Ministry in the Postmodern Matrix, *(Zondervan Publishing House, 2000);* Finding Faith *(Zondervan Publishing House, 1999);* A New Kind of Christian *(John Wiley and Sons, 2001); and* More Ready Than You Realize, *(Zondervan Publishing House, 2001).*

Brian's wife, Grace, is a consultant in teambuilding and human resource development. They have four children in their teens and twenties, one of whom is a cancer survivor. Brian's personal interests include ecology, fishing, hiking, kayaking, camping, music, art, and literature. His e-mail address is brianm@crcc.org.

CHAPTER

4

OUTWARD-FOCUSED PARTNERSHIPS

Connecting With Other Churches Beyond Church Walls

BY
TOM
PELTON

During the past ten years, millions of Christians of all denominations have come together on city streets to demonstrate their unity in Christ in the March for Jesus. We have organized marches, some as large as fifty thousand people, in more than fifteen hundred cities across the United States. Many of these marches are the largest and most diverse gatherings of the body of Christ these communities have ever seen.

The remarkable thing about these massive events is that they are not done with a massive budget or staff of professional organizers. They are not organized by national ministry or evangelistic crusades that come in to set up operations. Volunteers organize them at the grassroots level as expressions of growing partnerships among local churches. In some cases, they have been the catalyst for partnerships among churches that will continue to produce good fruit for years to come.

It has been a remarkable journey.

There is something unseemly about self-promotion. On the other hand, there is something about the crucible of cooperation that purifies our efforts. By working with others, an outward-focused church is able to serve the community without drawing attention to itself. It knows the power of remaining hidden. Working together is often a difficult process. It's sometimes easier to just "do your own thing," but the sacrifices we make to work in a relationship with others move us to a level of servanthood and humility not usually required by our individual efforts.

I have spent the past ten years meeting with pastors' groups across the nation as pastors mobilize their congregations to work together. In the process, I've learned a lot about how effective partnerships among local churches can be. I've also been fascinated by how these partnerships bring biblical balance to diverse leaders and deepen the spiritual impact of a citywide effort.

THE JOURNEY FROM INDEPENDENT TO INTERDEPENDENT

I grew up a "fighting fundamentalist." We were proud of being independent and heavy on the fundamental. We didn't like other denominations. We didn't even like other Baptists! I remember watching church members throw hymn books across the sanctuary at each other during a business meeting.

Unity was called ecumenicism, and to us that required a watered-down compromise of all we believed. We didn't want to be "polluted" by others. We feared that any association with those we disagreed with might imply our support for their "wrong" teachings. We were extremely fearful of anyone who didn't wear our label. Our forefathers had fought a bitter battle to defend some core distinctives that made our group of churches unique.

Outsiders had a hard time understanding how such small peripheral issues could become so divisive. But we were so highly suspicious of outsiders that any difference could represent hidden dangers. If your hairstyle is a bit too contemporary, who could know what horrible heresy might be lurking in your doctrine!

Our thinking was circular. For example, we believed that, if you didn't use the King James version of the Bible, you would compromise on other key issues and have fuzzy doctrine. If you were not rooted in strong doctrine, you might believe anything, which meant you could be one of those who change the Scripture to mean whatever they want. You deny the virgin birth, the Resurrection, and the Atonement. And if that were the case, you would worship a different Jesus and not really be a Christian but a part of the harlot church we are warned about in Revelation.

So we pretty much stayed to ourselves.

Fortunately, modern communication and information has made it more difficult for us to believe some of the misconceptions we held about one another.

I'm a channel surfer. I never particularly cared for *Jerry Springer*, but I have to admit a pause while surfing sometimes lasted the full program as I sat in amazement, watching what people would talk about on television. I've never liked Christian television either. When we got cable television, I sat and watched it for the first time. Some of the strangest people I had ever seen were talking about Jesus, so I had to see what was going on. It took awhile to get past the hair, the makeup, the lavish sets, and some far-out interpretations of Scripture, but I couldn't ignore the love for Jesus I shared with these people. In fact, the extreme difference made an impression on me. If people that far distant from what I believed and practiced could share my love for Jesus, there are certainly others I have rejected who are actually part of my family.

Later I was greatly surprised to discover Episcopalians who loved Jesus and were truly born again. I found charismatics who were stronger in biblical teaching than anyone I had known. I found Catholics who taught me about prayer, Presbyterians who were passionate about evangelism, Methodists who spoke in tongues, and Baptists who loved everybody! I discovered a family I never knew I had.

Many of us have made this journey from independence to interdependence—to a genuine affection for every part of the body of Christ and recognition that we are incomplete without each other. For me it happened on the street.

It was a hot, sunny day in Austin, Texas, and we were marching up Congress Avenue to the Capitol in that first March for Jesus. Getting two hundred churches of all denominations together in Austin was a major breakthrough. As far as the eye could see, people of all colors and ages held balloons and banners celebrating Jesus. We felt something that day. Small churches were no longer small; they were part of a big church. Big churches were no longer islands of isolation; they were partners in a shared vision of reaching an entire city. We had known these things could be but never realized it until we came face to face with who we really were.

Walking down that street, I acknowledged for the first time that these people were my brothers and sisters—even the ones I considered strange. I'd walked down church aisles before, but it was always to join a church of people who were exactly like me. I had always identified with those I agreed with and tried to distance myself from those who were part of the family—but different.

During the following weeks, pastors would meet for prayer each Tuesday morning and then go to breakfast together. In that prayer circle and around that breakfast table, we worked out a set of values that would guide our relationships. It would take years to live out the revelation we experienced on the street that day. But we could never again think only of the efforts of our individual congregations when we planned ministry to reach the city.

THE JOURNEY FROM "A CITY FOR MY CHURCH" TO "A CHURCH FOR MY CITY"

I don't know about you, but I know I tend to evaluate all things based on how they benefit me. I hate to admit it, but I tend to be self-centered. I know it's just me. If I'm in a group photograph, the first person I look for is me. I'll decide if it's a good or bad photo based on how *I* look!

When I was pastoring, I evaluated all things in my city based on how they benefited my church. I know, I know, it's just me. When I heard that a church was having problems, I secretly hoped some of the people would come over to our church. I actually sent out a letter once stating that our church was the best in town. I didn't think about the possibility that it was a put-down of every other church in town. The thought never occurred to me. I considered other churches my competition.

You might find this hard to believe, but I wasn't really there to serve the community. I came to the city because I considered it a great place to build the church of my dreams. I expected the city to serve me. So I built a big church but not a great one.

The problem is that my self-centeredness runs directly contrary to the kingdom Jesus offers. I never realized that the self-centeredness of my church had to be confronted as well.

"Do nothing out of selfish ambition or vain conceit, but in humility consider others better than yourselves. Each of you should look not only to your own interests, but also to the interests of others. Your attitude should be the same as that of Christ Jesus" Philippians 2:3-5.

The biblical admonitions to be Christlike that we preach to *people* apply to *churches* as well. My church should be as committed to the success of the church down the street as I am committed to my own church's success.

THE JOURNEY FROM EVANGELISM GOALS TO KINGDOM VALUES

It was praying for the city that got me into this mess. I was invited to join a group of pastors in prayer for revival in our city. About eight of us gathered every Tuesday morning at six, prayed for at least an hour, and then went to breakfast together.

Prayer times began to take an interesting turn. We had gathered to pray for the city. We had gathered to pray for the increase of our churches. We had gathered to pray for evangelism to reach every household. But as we prayed, it became obvious that God wanted to deal with the problems in our own hearts and lives. We found that there is a vast difference between launching another evangelistic campaign and facing the implications of living together in the kind of relationships that demonstrated the kingdom Jesus talked about. We wanted to evangelize the city; God wanted to advance his kingdom. And it had to begin in us. We discovered that this kind of evangelistic vision evangelizes the heart of the evangelist.

BENEFITS OF OUTWARD-FOCUSED PARTNERSHIPS

Outward-focused partnerships bring balance to extremes

These days, any pastor with the courage to pull together a church of any size probably has an obsessive-compulsive personality. At a seminar for CEOs of nonprofit organizations, a speaker lecturing on board-CEO relationships said, "You wouldn't be attending this seminar unless you were already one sick puppy." The energy that drives us toward success can also make us crazy when it's focused in the wrong direction. You don't drive a finishing nail with a sledgehammer. You don't want all the passion, power, vision, and drive of an apostolic leader focused on a small point of doctrine. That's how people end up dressed in robes and chanting on the hillside.

All kinds of leaders need to be reminded of the bigger picture so they can gain some perspective. Sometimes even the best leaders need to be confronted by someone they respect. The day-to-day relationship with other leaders on a peer level helps bring balance to leaders. They can receive from one another what they often cannot get from those within their congregation. We all need to realize that we need people around us whose different viewpoints help us put things in perspective when we become obsessed with a situation.

Outward-focused partnerships confront self-centeredness

Even the ministry we do in Christ's name can become self-serving. I never knew how self-centered I was until I tried to do things in partnership with other people. Believe it or not, they don't just go along with me when what I'm doing serves only me. To be effective in a partnership, I have to be truly committed to something that serves the interest of everyone involved.

Outward-focused partnerships require being Christlike

It's interesting that Jesus sent out his disciples two by two. Perhaps it was for their protection. Or could it be that Jesus set them up that way because ministering in partnership would require that they be Christlike? It seems not enough to Christ that the gospel is preached; apparently he wants it preached in a proper context. The message and the method must match. In fact Luke 9:21-23 suggests that Jesus would rather his name is preached in a context of self-sacrifice or not at all. "Jesus strictly warned them, do not tell this to anyone…Then he said to them all: 'If any man would come after me, he must deny himself and take up his cross daily and follow me.' "

Outward-focused partnerships encourage the church

There is something remarkable about God's kingdom that inspires us to something better. When we see it in action, it restores our hope. The kingdom way is simply the way things should be. When we see it demonstrated, it dispels the disillusionment that often comes when we observe life. The kingdom in action illustrates a better way than what we see happening in the world.

I've seen this hope come alive when people see churches partnering. People get inspired. I see a twinkle in their eyes. It's more than just a joyful moment; lightness is replacing a low-grade depression of the soul that comes when the church turns out to be just like all the other institutions of man. A demonstration of true kingdom servanthood and humility restores hope. The invisible kingdom Jesus talked about is not just a wonderful truth to ponder; life actually can be better than what we see every day. We must see this kingdom in operation, or we lose hope.

Outward-focused partnerships create opportunities to share strengths

Many of us have no idea what resources lie within the churches in our communities. Some churches have found partnership so rewarding that the partnerships have led to the merger of churches. In some cases, partnerships have led to planting churches together; in others the gifts stored up in one congregation have been released for the benefit of churches throughout the community.

ASPECTS OF RELATIONAL UNITY

Shared Leadership

Outward-focused partnerships require a different kind of leadership than the vertical structure most church leaders are accustomed to. When many strong leaders are involved, a horizontal leadership structure is needed, as well as a consultative style of leadership that can facilitate shared ownership. Shared leadership is becoming more common. In fact, these partnerships can become an excellent training ground for the kind of church leadership that will be required for the future. While a hierarchical leadership is often easily accepted by those who have been in church culture for years, the next generation and people coming from outside the church culture will relate better to the more horizontal leadership structure. Some emerging church leaders would argue that these more horizontal structures, while apparently divesting clergy of traditional control and power, are more effective in releasing and empowering lay people and multiplying ministry.

Leaders tend to think organizationally. Partnering churches and organizations are not looking for another organization to join; however they are interested in being part of a movement that maximizes their impact. The bottom line is that, when working beyond the congregation, we need leadership structures that stimulate and resource a movement rather than build an organization.

Friendship

God's kingdom is built on relationships. Leaders are finding there is no substitute for authentic friendships, and a partnership is where that kind of relationship is formed. I find groups of pastors who have become friends and then decided to do things together. Their friendship flows through everything they do. The friendship of a group of pastors in Austin, Texas, was the beginning of the March for Jesus that would affect their city and the entire nation. Those core relationships have led to numerous ministries within the city over the years.

Catalytic Events

Catalytic events can stimulate the formation of relationships among churches. These events help partnerships reach a productive stage. Outward-focused partnerships go beyond relationship to begin to actually function together. A truly outwardly focused church is not content to simply go deeper relationally. These relationships, like other human relationships, are nurtured by shared experiences and history. Events cultivate new relationships, nurture existing relationships, and help partners exercise their ability to function together. And besides, they're fun!

Core Competencies

Through relationships, churches can get to know one another and begin to draw from the core competency, or strength, of each part of the body. Forming the relationships, though, requires a willingness to see the strength of each part rather than its weakness. We all have weaknesses, and we'd all like to keep our weaknesses hidden. When churches focus on the weaknesses they see in others, they typically move away from prospective partners. When they learn to recognize each other's strengths, the same churches can begin to see all kinds of partnership possibilities. Every church regardless of size or inherent weakness, can become a valuable asset to the partnership because of the unique strengths it brings to the mix. Only after these core competencies have been identified and affirmed can weaknesses be dealt with. In fact, once their strengths are affirmed, churches often openly share weaknesses they had carefully hidden.

Shared Vision

Partnerships begin with relationship, but it's shared vision that allows partnerships to grow. Notice the word *shared.* Sometimes a particular leader's vision can become a catalyst for a partnership, but for the partnership to thrive, the vision must be shared. It can't be the vision of just one leader expecting others to support his vision. Whether the vision comes from a participant in the group, an outside ministry, or the group together, at some point it must be internalized by everyone in the partnership to the point that it becomes a shared vision. All must see themselves as servants of a shared vision rather than supporters of an organization, members of an alliance, committee members with responsibilities, or leaders on a platform. And all must feel an authentic passion for the common vision.

A prayerfully developed vision shared among a group of leaders creates a powerful partnership that can impact an entire community. Shared vision confronts personal ambition and transcends organizational structure. It is the driving force that moves a partnership forward and keeps it outwardly focused. An outward-focused partnership can demonstrate the kingdom so dramatically that it inspires an entire community.

PRACTICAL SUGGESTIONS

• *Change Your Leadership Structure*

Shared leadership requires a leadership structure that is bigger and broader than current structures. Rather than build an organization, the leadership structure for shared leadership needs to serve a movement. If a particular church is taking the initiative, that church must be especially careful to give away leadership, responsibility, and authority. Highly invested churches should realize that, because they are already committed, they should use leadership roles as a way to share ownership with others. Larger churches, in particular, should be very aware that, while their identity will win some support, it will alienate others and, in the long haul, can undermine the long-term success of the initiative.

A group of leaders of various churches and ministries should be at the head of the initiative, meeting regularly to plan and pray together and to help develop the broader identity of the initiative. These leaders must have a high level of trust and be able to challenge one another. Since these leaders are typically busy, their focus should be their relationship with one another and the broader issues of the initiative. They should appoint and empower others to focus on the tasks involved in the initiative and then oversee their progress.

• *Mobilize*

It's better to have lots of people doing lots of small tasks than a few people doing too much. It is actually best to develop as many volunteer positions as possible. Volunteer positions create ownership and allow more people to be involved. So break down the tasks into as many small pieces as possible.

The massive stadium events of the great evangelists operate on the principle that every person has a sphere of influence of about ten people. If you attend a Billy Graham event attended by forty thousand people, you will probably see a choir of four thousand. So if you want ten thousand people at an event, recruit one thousand volunteers and get them excited about getting their friends and family involved. Create as many volunteer titles and job descriptions as possible. Titles empower people for the task.

• *Meet*

Meetings are often where the work of the church gets

done. Don't hesitate to plan lots of meetings in preparation for mobilization. A carefully scheduled series of planning meetings on a timeline are motivational and exciting. They build momentum toward a goal. You'll find that much of the actual value of an event is the preparation for it. Meetings also are a great way to make sure progress is being made. There is nothing like the threat of public humiliation to motivate people to get done what they have been assigned to do!

• *Celebrate*

Outward-focused churches know the value of gathering for celebration. Shared values and shared vision are what bring churches together. Celebrations are a great way to celebrate those values and lift up the shared vision.

• *Facilitate Levels of Commitment*

Recognize that some churches will be committed core partners, others will be somewhat committed, and yet others will only participate in the partnership initiative from time to time. Facilitate all levels of involvement.

• *Release Visionaries and Activists*

Church leaders who want to reach a city should recruit business and professional leaders. There are successful people who are not being challenged by traditional church leadership roles but who will thrive on ministry into the broader community. Lay people have great ideas and untapped potential to lead ministry that extends beyond traditional church structures. When identified and supported by church leaders, these individuals can work wonders in a community.

About the Author

Tom Pelton is the founder of *March for Jesus USA*, a nonprofit organization that facilitates Christian unity and community involvement. He helped start *We Care America* to unite and strengthen compassion ministry. Recently he established *Jesus Day* to mobilize churches to feed the hungry, care for fatherless children, and reach out to suffering people. Tom is also a founding member of the *Mission America Coalition* executive board. This coalition now includes sixty denominations and three hundred faith-based organizations.

A heart for church unity based on outward ministry to the needy has led him to involvement with the *National Prayer Committee*, the *International Reconciliation Coalition* and other organizations working toward unity, reconciliation, and community-wide mobilization.

Tom's background includes twenty years of pastoral ministry in churches ranging from Baptist and Episcopal to nondenominational. He and his wife, Theresa, have two children, Rachel and Timothy.

A GOD-SIZED TRANSFORMATION

Helping a Traditional Church See Beyond Church Walls

BY STEPHEN L. AYERS

W hen the Spirit of God is loosed among people, something God-sized is bound to happen. It did at Hillvue Heights Church in Bowling Green, Kentucky.

Hillvue Heights is always looking outward. We believe that people who do not have a relationship with God through Jesus Christ are dead in sin. We believe that people who receive Jesus Christ are forgiven of that sin and come to a full and abundant new life. Death and life are what Hillvue Heights Church is about. All around us, we see "dead people"—people who do not have a relationship with Jesus Christ, who are dying in their sins. Our vision of the new life that is possible for such people urges us to be outward-focused—to spread the good news of Jesus Christ.

Hillvue Heights Church hasn't always been this way. In fact, the church itself has been transformed from death to life. In 1991, Hillvue Heights was a typical Baptist church. It's earlier prosperous years had come to an end, and the church stood near death, with fewer than fifty people attending and a debt of $450,000. The people had to decide whether they were going to live or die. They decided to die, so they might live.

DRINKING FROM GOD'S CUP

First I must tell you that the Hillvue Heights Church was built, not on church growth methods or pretty songs, but on a heartfelt conviction that *people are dying without Jesus and we must take the message of Jesus to those people.* It is truly that simple. However, dying in order to live again isn't easy.

To tell the story of how Hillvue Heights Church learned to do ministry by being in Jesus, I'll describe the four cups we learned to drink from: the cup of death, the cup of possibility, the cup of joy, and the cup of celebration.

THE CUP OF DEATH

Hillvue Heights chose to die to its old ways and to be risen with Christ in a new way. As pastor of the Hillvue Heights Church, I was the first one who had to experience Galatians 2:20. I had to die to my preconceived notions of what it means to be a pastor.

After seminary, I was all excited, thinking that I'd likely arrive in a four- or five-hundred-member church with a starting salary of at least forty thousand. I felt I had paid my dues within the Baptist system by pastoring small churches where no one else really wanted to go. I just knew God would place me where I could prosper.

God did that, but first I had to die to who I was and what I was about. I was thinking about a career; God taught me that I had a calling. I had to become a minister of the gospel of Jesus, a person who was willing to share the good news of Jesus Christ, no matter the context. I had to *die* to the social-climbing ladder of the Baptist structure and go where God wanted me to go.

I knew that God had placed me in the Hillvue Heights Church. I knew that the odds of succeeding there seemed impossible. I also knew that as a twenty-six-year-old dreamer I had neither the skill, the personality, nor the insight to cause this church to live. But when I died to pastoring my way, God began to pastor his way.

Willing to risk

The people at Hillvue Heights were willing to take some risks, and as we began our journey on March 10, 1991, we all began to drink from the cup of death. Before any church can become an outward-focused church, it has to die as a church that *does* business and begin to live as a church that *is* ministry. The first thing that had to die was the name of the church. People out there who had never been to church just held too many preconceived notions about what a Baptist was. And I was more concerned about people becoming followers of Jesus than I was about their becoming Baptists. So we removed *Baptist* from our name. When we were discussing a further name change, Bettye Lois Smith chose to die and drink from the cup of death. She suggested we keep "Hillvue Heights Church" as the name so that, when the church was thriving, people would remember it as a place that had been resurrected. She and the others were willing to die so that Jesus could live.

As we began to drink from the cup of death, we died to a lot of things. We died to the past. We quit worrying about how things had been done, who had done them, and where they had been done. People carried a lot of hurt, a lot of pain and anguish. But we had die to all that. We had to let the history hit the ground, so that new life could spring up. I remember that first sermon as if it were yesterday. I preached from Philippians 3:13-14 and repeated Paul's words: "Brothers, I do not consider myself yet to have taken hold of it. But one thing I do: forgetting what is behind and straining toward what is ahead, I press on..."

As we began to change, Galatians 2:20 resounded in our spirits: "I have been crucified with Christ and I no longer live, but Christ lives in me..." The people at Hillvue Heights Church realized that, if Jesus did not live inside its body, opening the doors to the community was irrelevant.

Becoming more

Before we could open the door, we had to drink from the cup of death, dying to who we were, so we could become who God wanted us to be. But death is not easy. We decided that to be more outward-focused we had to quit doing Sunday evening worship and do other things—get together in small groups in people's homes, for example, or hang out where people hung out on Sunday evening.

For staunch supporters of that southern Sunday-night-worship tradition, this was a painful death. When one lady came to me and said, "I cannot believe you have cancelled Sunday evening service," I asked her for a favor. I said, "Give it four weeks, and if it doesn't work for you, I will personally come back on Sunday evening and preach to you, even if you're the only one here." On the third week, I asked her if I needed to prepare a Sunday evening sermon for the next week. She exclaimed, "I have never felt better on Monday—*never* felt better on Monday!"

We in the church began to realize that we practiced some things just because we had practiced them. It was time to quit practicing religion and start living in a relationship that led to resurrected lives in the community of faith. Yes, Hillvue Heights Church drank from the cup of death. We let our way of doing things die so we could pick up *God's* way of doing things.

Three things were resurrected from the deaths. First, we accepted each other in love. Even from the first day of worship, there was an acceptance of people and a new day. Second, we learned that we were all going to be different and that was OK. We died to the concept that everybody had to like everything for us to have church. When we died to that concept, God resurrected a love that said, "Even though we don't agree, we will still win people to Jesus. You win people to Jesus in your expression; I will win people to Jesus in my expression; but through every expression, we will experience the resurrection power of knowing Jesus as our Lord and Savior." The third resurrection was this: everyone was welcome to give up his or her former life and die in order to have a new life. As we drank from the cup of death, others from the community surrounding Bowling Green began to realize that they, too, could have a new life.

Demonstrating new life

The church began to demonstrate this new life. After we began to die to our way of doing things, the church began to grow. We didn't visit door-to-door. We didn't advertise or use marketing strategies. We didn't have all the bells and whistles of polished praise and worship. We sang songs with the spirit of welcome and the spirit of hope. We sang old hymns. We sang anthems. We sang choir specials. Sometimes we sang on key; sometimes we sang off key. But whatever we sang, we sang it with resurrection power.

For some reason, when people came and sat in that chapel called Hillvue Heights Church, they began to sing. They began to sing the song of resurrection because they realized they were dead without Jesus. And we began to realize the mission of the Church was to live a resurrected life in Jesus. We learned to work together, paint together, cook together, and camp out together. None of us had a lot of money, but what money we had, we gave it together, and together we began to be resurrected.

I never will forget the night the resurrection was illustrated to my family and me during our first Easter celebration at Hillvue Heights. For our worship experience on Good Friday, we had set a table at the altar. The table held a loaf of bread and cups of grape juice. For two hours, groups of people came and went. People sat around the table, broke bread, drank the cup, and remembered Jesus. It was not planned this way, but as different groups came and went, nobody sat at the head of the table. It was as if Jesus himself was there at the head of the table throughout the entire night, and he really was. As each one of us around that table reflected on Jesus' dying for us, we began to realize that we too must die so we might live.

It is that resurrected life that allows the doors to be thrown open at Hillvue Heights Church with the screaming call, "Come and die so that you might live anew in Jesus." And we continue to sip from the cup of death. We've learned to die to anger, jealousy, bitterness, and envy; for if you open the doors of the church and all that people find is another organization, they will never be satisfied. Paul said,

"I have joined the sufferings of Jesus, so I might know the power of his resurrection" (Philippians 3:10, paraphrased). The resurrection will promote itself. It did at Hillvue. People came to see what an alive church looked like, and the church began to grow.

THE CUP OF POSSIBILITY

In these growing moments, we also began to drink from the cup of possibility. We began to realize that we weren't a dead church. Jesus said that we could do all things through him. People began to wake up. Instead of having the pre-prescribed ministries of the Baptist church, we began to ask crazy questions, such as, "What can you do?" Ministries began to develop. For example, people shared their faith in lake ministries as they played on the nearby lake. Golf-course ministries were big in the early days of Hillvue, as those who played golf would simply go and play on Sunday afternoons and invite other golfers to check out church.

One golfer was reached this way after his fiancée started coming to Hillvue and asked him to come to church. He had met some of the Hillvue golfers on the golf course, so he decided to try the church. He came one morning, and then he quit playing golf on Sunday mornings. When his four-some buddies asked where he'd been, he exclaimed, "I can't invite you to come to church with me, because if you go, you'll never play golf again on Sunday morning." One of the foursome came one Sunday to get his clubs out of his buddy's car in Hillvue's parking lot. The car was locked, so he thought, "I'll just go in there and get him." When he saw our people packed in a chapel and dressed like he was, he began to listen. He became overwhelmed by the Holy Spirit.

He forgot his clubs and his Sunday morning golf game. Now the entire used-to-be-Sunday-morning-foursome attends worship regularly!

When you begin to drink from the cup of possibility, ministry is not seen in the church as much as it's seen in the community. Hillvue's story is not about a pristine building or a great church-growth methodology. It's a story of a group of people saying, "We can do it through Jesus Christ, who strengthens us."

Seeing the possibilities

Praise music was not something we started so people would come to church; praise music was something that started happening because people *were* coming to Hillvue and experiencing the resurrection power and the hope of possibility. A man named Ed Norman, an old friend of mine, came and played the piano the second Sunday I was there. He mesmerized everybody with sounds of hope and joy. Ed eventually became our praise and worship pastor, and our worship began to embody the spirit of Hillvue. Every Sunday morning, people sensed a hope in possibility. And more people began to come to see what was happening. Before long, we ran out of room!

Possibility attracts people. About our third or fourth year at Hillvue Heights Church, a common hope was that a parking space might possibly be available. A hopeful spirit pervaded the church. One person who now is one of our leaders first came to church because he had never seen a group of people standing on a lawn waiting to get into a church. What was inside? The possibility of a new life.

As we drank from the cup of possibility, the hope of God came among us. People found it possible to give up drugs and alcohol and to live life free of those addictions.

People found it possible to heal marriages. In fact, one couple came to Hillvue Heights Church *divorced*. Six months after participating in a community of possibility, they were remarried. They have remained remarried for seven years, and are expecting their third child. God's possibilities outweighed the world's consequences.

As we drank from the cup of possibility, we saw people who had been labeled as useless, hopeless, and nonproductive become the creative ministers of this new day. One of my closest brothers in the church is a friend named Jimmy who has long hair, earrings, and tattoos. When Jimmy found the possibility of God in his life, he gave up a life of drug abuse and roaming and found direction in Jesus. He now spends all his time, wherever he is, sharing the good news of Jesus Christ. The Sunday following Jimmy's experience of new life, he brought to church ten "dead people" with whom he had shared Jesus during the week. Jimmy points dead people to Jesus every day.

Existing for a purpose

At Hillvue Heights, people were changing, and other people saw it. All around the city, they were saying, "Something's going on in that church." We knew it had to be from God, because the religious were upset and the unrighteous were coming through our doors. We simply threw open the doors of the church and said, "Hey listen, we're coming back to life. Why don't you bring your life here and come back to life with us?"

As we drank from the cup of possibility, the vision of the church became clear. We had become a community of faith that existed, lived, and breathed for the city of Bowling Green and the community of south-central Kentucky. Our vision is to lead people to a relationship with Jesus Christ, to show people that Jesus can heal the wounds of their sin, and to let people know that they too can become ministers of grace. We keep this vision in front of us to remember why we exist.

THE CUP OF JOY

In the cup of possibility, we found the cup of joy. We started being joyful before we realized it! Worship experiences would last way past an hour, but nobody cared because the joy of the Lord was among us. In my own life, I began to love people more, to hug them as they came through the door and "high five" them at the altar after they met Jesus. We had long-haired people, short-haired people, business people, blue-haired people (old and young)—all people who were attracted by the joy of the Lord. If I could encourage you to do one thing in your church, it would be this: Drink from the cup of joy. Be joyful about everything.

We were joyful inside our church. We didn't have great facilities or parking, but we had the joy of the Lord. We threw open the doors of the church to the city though we didn't have enough room for the city. But through Jesus Christ, we had enough joy to give them.

I would ask people, "Why do you come here?" They would tell me, "There's something in here. I've never enjoyed myself this much." Some of the most macho Southern men would come with their wives, gritting their teeth to make it through a church service so their wives might be pleased, and end up crying with the joy of the Lord through a whole service. They'd ask, "When am I gonna quit crying?"

I'd have to say, "I don't know, bro'; it's part of the package."

Sharing the joy of the Lord

The joy of the Lord became more evident as people began to share Jesus with their friends. We've never had an organized visitation program. We just let the joy of the Lord loose, and it got so loose that people told their friends about the joy of knowing of Jesus. Sharing our faith wasn't a requirement; it was just a natural response to drinking from the cup of joy. We shared our faith by standing in the parking lot and talking—long hours after service was over. And sometimes that sharing of faith even meant interrupting schedules inside the church! The joy of the Lord attracts people. Nehemiah 8:10 says it best: "The joy of the Lord is your strength." At Hillvue Heights Church, we didn't have much money. We didn't have a whole lot of fancy, flashy things to show people. But we had an irrepressible joy.

We started in a sanctuary that would only hold about three hundred fifty folks, but we were able to get four or five hundred in when we counted the people in the foyer, the stage area, and the hallways. In the summertime, some people even stood outside. The Spirit of the Lord would fall on the congregation, and many people would come to the altar to receive Jesus Christ. Everyone would celebrate, and many would have their hands in the air. We don't even know when that began happening. You know, as a Baptist church, we were supposed to be seated; we were supposed to be still. But when the joy of the Lord gets upon you, sometimes you have the joy of the Lord exploding in you before you realize it, and sometimes you have your hands in the air.

On one particularly hot August day, several people were meeting Jesus, and the service had gone way past its scheduled time. One of our pastors walked outside to the crowd waiting for the next worship service. He told them that the

Spirit of the Lord was moving and that people were receiving Christ. The crowd cheered, prayed, and began to sing songs of joy. Then in the next moment, the choruses that were being sung inside the chapel were being sung outside as well! The joy of the Lord had spread to the crowd outside.

We often heard, "I've never seen anything like this." I'd say, "Good, I'm glad to hear you say that. Jesus must definitely be here." People said things like that when Jesus walked the earth. One morning when a child was baptized, a close friend of the child stood up and began to clap and celebrate the experience of baptism. Since most of the people in the chapel were not "church-trained" and didn't know what to do at church, everybody stood up and joined him in clapping and celebrating. Before long, after every baptism, our people gave standing ovations celebrating the joy of new life in Christ. I'm thankful that we're a church that's still clapping, because many people who are dead in their sins still need to be baptized into the life of Jesus Christ.

THE CUP OF CELEBRATION

We have learned what it means to open our arms to the city and say, "Y'all come. Jesus loves you so much. He'll give you a new life." This is the cup of celebration, and we have learned how to celebrate.

"I invite you to dance; I hope you dance," sings LeeAnn Womack in the title song, "I Hope You Dance" (by Mark Sanders and Tia Sillers), of her 2000 CD. It's a song that should echo in the halls of the church. At Hillvue, we learned to dance. We learned to celebrate. We learned to move. We learned to talk. We learned to be still. We learned to celebrate life, love, and simply Jesus being there. We began to clap during the singing. We began to stand at unusual times. And sometimes people even come to the altar to meet Jesus in the midst of praise. We get so caught up in Jesus that others see him being released in us. We've learned to celebrate. We've learned to dance.

Learning to dance

A few years ago in the midst of worship, a group of four- and five-year-old girls began dancing and twirling at the front of the church, their dresses flowing in the breeze. One of them was my daughter. Mothers started forward, concerned that their children were disturbing the worship experience. I stopped the mothers and said, "I'm not going to tell you what to do with your child. However, my little girl likes to twirl everywhere she goes. What could be the worst thing about this? The children could grow up and remember going to church and having a wonderful time. What harm could there be in that?" I realized that these children were drinking from the cup of celebration. Though they didn't know how to be "churched," they knew how to dance with Jesus. I remember asking Jesus, "Will you teach me to dance like my daughter knows how to dance? Will you teach me to celebrate and to be more concerned about your celebration than my exercise of ministry?"

The Lord has taught me more than once in the past ten years that his celebration is greater than my organization and that his celebration will draw those who are dead into life. My organization will only herd people through another set of informational hearings. Jesus Christ enters into the heart and the soul of the human being and begins the celebration.

Our first "Godstock" celebrations are a good example. We take the whole church camping, and people worship and camp together in a state park for a weekend. It is here that I have learned the community of church. It is here that I have learned to live with brothers and sisters. It is here that I have learned to preach into the wind of the community. It is here where we throw open our doors as an outward-focused church. It is here that we say, "Come, worship and celebrate with us, camp with us, eat with us, cook with us, but most of all, come be in Jesus with us." And they've come.

Celebrating in sadness

Celebration also involves holding the hands of sorrow. Sometimes celebration is not as happy as the baptisms or the dance at the altar. I have celebrated when a friend's father committed suicide. I tasted the salty, sorrowful part of the cup, but we celebrated that Jesus was there, even in our sorrow. And when one of our young people went to be with Jesus after a tragic car accident, many from our church felt both the sorrow and the celebration while gathered in the halls of that emergency room. In the midst of the tragedy of death, I was reminded once again—*life to death, death to life*—the rhythm of God's celebration. God says in Ecclesiastes 3:4 there is "a time to mourn and a time to dance." Even in our mourning, the dance of Jesus is still among us.

PICKING UP THE CUP

I hope that you've been encouraged to die to a normal way of pastoring and to come alive to Jesus' way of pastoring. Check your Bible and see: Jesus did as much ministry while passing through town as he did while teaching. What do people find when they pass through your church? Do they find that you have died to your old ways and systems and picked up Jesus' way: a way of welcome, a way of love, a way of hope, a way of possibility? Truly all things are possible through Jesus Christ. Nothing in our church could have happened without Jesus directing it. There was no method. There was no drive. We had to depend on Jesus. The Spirit of God had to bring the church to life before it could look out and say to the world, "Come and live with us."

After we had died to ourselves and begun to live in the possibilities of God, we experienced the joy of the Lord, and we have learned to receive *all* people with joy! As you look into the city, don't focus on all its evils and ills. Quit looking at the works of the devil, and start injecting the joy of the Lord right into the midst of the devil's song.

Dance! Dance! Dance with Jesus. Dance with him at the ballgame, at the supermarket, and as you drive down the road. Let people know that you have a dancing partner, the one who is life! Celebrate life, mourn, hope, and live. The world has grown tired of our veneer Christianity and our plastic church. The world is hungry for a church that will drink from God's cup.

When we drink from the cup during the Lord's Supper, we remember that unless we die to self we cannot live for Jesus. As we drink, we drink possibility into our lives—the possibility that we can do all things through the One who strengthens us. We drink the joy of the Lord, even in moments of sorrow. We drink from the cup to remember that God is celebrating with us. We drink from that cup because God is God.

Pick up the cup of death, the cup of possibility, the cup of joy, and the cup of celebration, celebrating God's life to the community. What the world needs to see is not an organization; the world needs to see the Spirit of God intermingled in the twisted strands of our lives. I invite you to be a church that drinks from the cups that bring new life. May God bless you as you hold up your cup and offer this toast to heaven: "Lord Jesus, I remember you—your death, your possibility, your joy, your celebration, and your life. Amen."

ABOUT THE AUTHOR

Dr. Stephen L. Ayers believes that the church is hope for the world today. Under his leadership, Hillvue Heights Church in Bowling Green, Kentucky, has grown from thirty people to several thousand in just ten years. He is a graduate of Western Kentucky University, Southern Baptist Theological Seminary, and Drew University. His adventures include loving his wife, Elizabeth, and kids, twelve-year-old Blake and eight-year-old Claci; riding Harleys; and water-skiing. The Cross and Resurrection daily take him on new adventures.

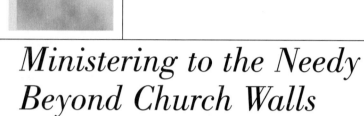

CHAPTER

6

FIRED UP!

Ministering to the Needy Beyond Church Walls

BY
DOUG
ROE

After a year and a half of what I considered utter failure as a church planter, I prayed a desperate prayer: "God, open a door for me—any door you choose. You open it, and I will walk through it."

If I'd had an idea what God had in mind, I probably would have put some conditions on my prayer. But amazingly, as only he can do, God began to answer my prayer immediately. The following day, I received a call from a woman I'd recently met whose sister was a long-term patient at a state mental hospital in the Dayton, Ohio, area. "Karen" had been in and out of institutions since she was a teenager. The mental conditions she suffered and the medications she took filled pages of medical reports.

I didn't realize it on my first visit, but Karen was to become my first of many "patients" at this institution. She seemed incorrigible on the surface. All I knew to do was to offer a prayer. The more she spoke of her many hang-ups, the less faith I had, so I simply offered to pray what I call "soaking" prayers—extended prayers that last five or more minutes. When I finished praying, she didn't seem remarkably moved by my efforts, but I did offer to return the following Tuesday, and she liked that idea.

When I returned, I was met not only by Karen but also by a handful of her friends. I had a quick inspiration. I pulled out of my briefcase an index card, wrote on it "Free Prayer," and placed it on a wooden table. It was kind of like Lucy's approach to advertising in the *Peanuts* comic strip, but instead of charging five cents, I did it for free.

Karen's friends had similar stories and situations. Most had been hospitalized for a long time. They were on a multitude of medications, and they all seemed hopeless. Pretty quickly I figured out that my role was to be a dispenser of hope. So every Tuesday I returned, placed my card on the table, and went to work on the long line of hope-impaired residents.

One day things took an unexpected turn. Karen made an announcement: "The doctors have declared me well—at least well enough to be moved to a half way house."

Curiously, that very week the hospital administrator approached me, introduced himself, and asked, "Say, who are you anyway?" You see, I had never asked permission to do any of this. I was following my motto: Jump and the net will appear! It had appeared for a full year, and the hospital situation had gone wonderfully. When he found out that I wasn't certified to do social work, he promptly asked me to leave! But that was OK; Karen was getting out.

SECRET TO SUCCESS: BUY A CEMETERY PLOT

Staying power. One of the first principles I learned about church planting while doing an internship with Steve Sjogren at the Vineyard Community Church in Cincinnati was, "When you find the city you are going to plant in, the first thing you do is buy a cemetery plot." That sounds a little morose, but it makes a powerful statement of commitment to a city and its people. That's why the first thing my wife and I did when we came to Dayton was make a lifelong commitment by buying burial plots. It was a good thing, because our commitment was severely tested right from the beginning.

We started on the northwest side of town with a nice group of people. They liked us, and we liked them, but from the beginning the mix didn't seem quite right. These people had their financial act together. On day one, they offered us a facility with great access to a major freeway. It all seemed just right. Then one day the yogurt hit the fan. They called my overseer and reported, "We like the Vineyard movement. We just don't like Doug."

As we parted ways, they suggested I do something more suited to my abilities, like a job in a grocery store. So I did. Still, I knew that God had called me to minister to people in Dayton. Plus I had those burial plots.

The handful of people who did like me (including my family!) moved our small group across town. I worked at the grocery store. (My specialty was setting up end-of-the row displays. There's an art to it; and I was good!) I began to pray for an open door so I could reach out to the people of our city. As I looked back at what went wrong with my first attempt in Dayton, all I could figure out was that I needed to increase the amount of energy I was spending on ministering to the needy. The only problem was that I didn't have any money to spend on ministry to the poor.

Then it hit me: Go into debt to minister to the needy! During the next few weeks, I activated half a dozen of the credit-card offers that came in the mail with promises of special, super-low interest rates. I decided to experiment, and I found that the more I invested in the needy, the stronger and more outward our struggling new church grew. While I was a little scared about my experiment, I was also incredibly excited. Now that I look back, I think it probably would have been prudent to tell my wife about the credit-card part. She found out…and eventually understood.

VISA WAS MY FRIEND

From the time of my epiphany about investing more in the needy, I began to share my vision with our tiny, new congregation. I made it clear, "We are going to be about ministering to the needy." Our goal was to come up with a new idea for creatively caring for the needy each week. As you might guess, some of our ideas were pretty decent and some weren't all that great.

We began an annual Barbecue Dayton which now attracts thousands of needy folks for fun, food, and even pony rides. I think every child needs to ride a pony at least once. Our extensive ministry to kids in need of school supplies goes on throughout the school year. On the other hand, the watermelon giveaway almost became a free-for-all because of the way we handed out the melons. And there was the neighborhood cleanup; it seemed like a good idea, but it sent a message that we thought their neighborhood was dirty and they needed suburban people to come down and lend a hand.

Our approach to starting a ministry to the needy was Ready, Fire, Aim! We bought coolers, barbecue grills, food to give away, trailers to carry things, rakes, squeegees, and dozens of other implements of service. It wasn't long before more than $35,000 had been charged to the Visa card.[1]

We learned quickly that those we served didn't necessarily come to church once they were served. But along the way, we discovered that an awful lot of people want to be a part of a church that cares for the needy. Slowly, surely the church began to grow. People began to relate to the vision that we had set out to embrace fully. That was ten years—and two thousand weekend attendees ago. And we are still a center for ministry to the needy.

> "...along the way, we discovered that an awful lot of people want to be a part of a church that cares for the needy."

TOUCHED WITH FIRE

Some years ago, my wife, Marcie, observed something interesting about most women and men who have a strong heart for outreach and evangelism. I know it sounds a bit odd, but try to be open to this observation. Marcie noticed that adults who have an unusual heart for outreach were often very curious about fire when they were children. That's not to say that they were full-scale pyromaniacs or that they were constantly lighting things up. But they were somewhat mesmerized by the power of fire—at least they were more impressed with its power than most.

During the past several years, I have done my own unofficial, unscientific study on "Marcie's Fire/Outwardness Theory," asking people who are highly motivated to be outwardly focused if they played with fire as kids. I've been amazed. After they recover from the blunt question, their jaws drop, they burst out with laughter, and they ask, "How did you know?"

Her theory certainly holds true in my life. When I was a

kid, back in the days when leaf-burning was allowed, I would volunteer to rake the leaves just so I could light them up at the end! I didn't so much "play" with fire. I respected it greatly. It is one of the most powerful forces on earth. It has great potential to do good when handled correctly.

I've begun to examine the parallels between fire and passion for the lost. Here are fiery discoveries I've made during the past ten years:

Everybody wants to be friends with those who are generous to the poor

I never set out to build a large church. Most of my favorite large churches across America—the ones that are worth learning from—didn't set out to be large. Numbers don't matter much to them, and numbers certainly don't matter much to me. However, numbers do tell a story—a story of momentum. It's for that reason alone that I report to you the numbers who have found their way to my church in Dayton.

We started out as a ragtag group of mostly misfit folks. We weren't the pretty people who had it all together, but we had in common a heart for giving.

It took us awhile to figure out why we were called to give to the needy. At first we thought it was to somehow "cure" the needy. But we have never succeeded in getting the people we served to come to our meetings in any significant numbers. We've tried all sorts of gimmicks to get them to come to church. For example, we'd offer to drive them to and from meetings, but they wouldn't be at the pickup point.

After awhile (actually, it took a few years), we figured out what this parable we were living out was all about. We weren't to come close to poor people to get them to attend our church. We were simply to care for the poor—with no strings attached—period. Most importantly, we were to be around poor people regularly and allow their lives to overlap ours. We were to allow their lives to touch us with the power and presence of the kingdom that resides in the needy. Once we figured it out, the lesson was worth the effort: We were the ones who were supposed to be changed by our ministry to the poor, not the other way around.

In spite of the fact that very few of the people we served came to our church, a funny thing happened along the way to learning our lessons on fire building. As we became outward-focused, we discovered that regular folks from around Dayton began to show up at our place. They were saying, more or less, "I may not be poor myself, but I want to care for the poor. I want to be a part of a place that cares for the poor. That's my heart." Our numbers began to grow as people identified with our heart for the needy. What a surprising discovery!

People are attracted to fire—anytime, any place.

The original thinker-philosopher-leader of the Burning Man project that attracts some thirty thousand artsy followers to the Black Rock Desert near Reno, Nevada, each Labor Day weekend has said, "Fire is the primal attractant."[2]

Perhaps that's why Acts 2 tells us that God birthed the church with tongues of fire. Throughout the Bible, fire is a metaphor for the power and presence of God's Spirit. But fire isn't just a biblical concept. There's nothing like a roaring fireplace on a cold winter's night to cause people to gather for conversation or just to hang out. We've all experienced the magnetic effect that a fireplace has in a large open room. Hearts open. Dreams begin to expand. Encouragement comes.

God starts fires with regular people

I'm just an average person. I was raised in a blue-collar

Dayton family, one that never learned to get the subject-predicate thing straight. My family would say, "Yesterday we was going out to..." That's just the way some people talk in Dayton. I call myself Charlie Brown. I can only be myself. My church is filled with "normal" people (and even a few abnormal people!). They don't see themselves as particularly skilled or qualified to do what they've stepped out to do with the needy.

I have found that many people are waiting for a phenomenal experience before they deem themselves ready to take on the big thing God has for them to do. They are waiting for "the call," as though some sort of mystical experience is waiting for them just around the corner. I disagree with that sort of thinking. I've never had a big "call" to anything I've done. I've never had a dramatic call to come to Dayton. I've never felt a big call to go into church planting or even to care for the poor. For the most part, I'm just convinced from reading Scripture and seeing the compelling evidence of the need at hand—that's what drives me forward.

I say, "Give up your conditions. Go forward—no matter what!" God wants to use ordinary, available people. God will faithfully equip us as we are faithful to just show up to do his bidding. As we are faithful, he will change our hearts in the process. As an aftereffect, the harvest we seek will happen.

Everyone should fail at starting a fire

I don't have much formal education, but the education I do have I've gotten mostly from the school of failure. I'm a big movie buff. One of the movies I have been taken by in recent years is *Cast Away* with Tom Hanks. A good deal of the first part of the movie shows Tom Hanks discovering the many ways to start a fire that *don't work*. As a veteran fire-starter, I felt enormously frustrated as I watched him struggle with the dozens of ineffective ways to fire things up when you don't have matches. But it was glorious to see him succeed at long last and to watch him dance around the flames, singing "Come on, baby, light my fi-r-re!" Based on my experiences with starting a ministry to the needy in Dayton, I identified with his struggles with the 101 ways to start a fire that didn't work.

Success is greatly overemphasized in the modern church. I've told my story to churches around the country, and it seems to me that the prevailing attitude of today's church is that success is the mark of God's favor. Success is great when it's from the Lord, but in my experience, success is most often built on the knowledge we've gleaned through failure.

Most of my favorite pastors and the churches I consider the best across America aren't all that well-known and aren't necessarily large. However, they all have learned powerful lessons about leadership from failure. Regardless of your size, failure is a powerful teacher. Failure is good for you in so many ways. I recommend you relish it and learn from it when it comes your way.

Authentic fires never start in an instant

I'm skeptical of quick successes.

My impatience made me a mediocre fire starter when I was in the Boy Scouts. When I was finally able to get a fire going, I did it by starting with small, dry twigs and then adding larger twigs, small sticks, larger sticks, and, finally, a full-fledged log. At long last, I'd have a fire.

God wants us to give care to others one week past the point when we think we ought to throw in the towel. God wants us to go out to minister whether anyone shows up or not. The needy have taught me to never, ever quit—even when all the forces around seem to be working against my best efforts. Resources may be low to nonexistent, which has certainly been the case for me many times. But few resources isn't an excuse for not moving toward the needy.

And weather may not cooperate. When we started doing ministry to the needy on a regular basis, it rained every time we stepped out to do a project. For a season, there would be a downpour every time! But we learned not to let that stop us.

One Saturday we had planned to do a carwash to raise money for the needy and, as usual, the rains came. We thought, "Who in their right mind would want to have a car washed when it's raining?" A couple of hearty souls showed up in spite of the weather. I said, "Pull your car out here; let's wash your car anyway and see what happens." Something amazing happened—other drivers pulled in to have their cars washed for free, even as the rain came down.

From that day on, we've consistently had great weather for our outreaches. No kidding! I can't prove it, but I think we made a spiritual breakthrough that day. Something spiritual had been causing it to literally rain on our parade every time we showed up. But the rain stopped when we pushed past the "I quit" barrier.

It's much the same as the famous "wall" that runners face after so many miles of running. I ride bikes quite a bit. I know that if I can endure past the ten-mile mark I will be able to make it to the fifteen-mile mark and ultimately complete a round-trip total of thirty miles.

It doesn't matter so much what we do as long as we love people

So often the tendency in the modern church is to be program-centered—to be looking for the brilliant program that's going to set the world aflame. I've found that there is no shortage of decent ideas or programs. The shortage is always in decent actions. It's never about the magic program. It's always about the power of heart.

A few months ago, I went to Mexico City with some friends and visited an orphanage that cares for kids who have been addicted to inhalants (a common problem in Mexico). The Christian-based orphanage, Ministerios de Amor, has gotten national attention because of its comprehensive care for these beautiful kids. Thanks to this program, they are housed, fed, and clothed—a first for many of them. But the day we were there, it wasn't the giving of food that impressed the kids.

I happened to bring my Palm Pilot with me. Some of the children were curious about this piece of electronics, so I typed the name of one of the children into the device. I pointed to the name and read it out loud. They looked at me as though I had done something magical. Quickly dozens of residents gathered. Stymied, I asked the director what the big deal was. "This is perhaps the first time these kids have seen their names written anywhere. Virtually every time they've heard their name it's been in a totally negative context. This is very special to them." The leaders of the group home explained that seeing and hearing their names in a positive way meant more to the kids than food or any programming we could have offered them that day.

We tend to be overly concerned with technique these days. But people are smart. They can always see past the externals. They can see the motivation behind what we are doing. There is little substance to the external stuff. It's the motivation of the heart that really matters, and that always shines through loud and clear.

Being able to listen attentively to anyone, of any mental capacity and of any background, and being able to connect—that's where it's at. Love bypasses all the externals, no matter what the differences may be.

We don't yet know what we don't know—so learn to ask the right questions

As I approach my fiftieth birthday, I am more aware than ever of how precious little I know about keeping the fire going, about ministry, about life, and about people. It seems that the older I get the less I know—or at least, the more I am aware of what I don't know. So I keep on asking questions.

Look for the spark, not the blazing fire

When I started in ministry to the needy, God put in my heart a desperation to do whatever it would take to go forward, including an openness to going to an institution for the mentally impaired. I have found that God is almost always with the small, the overlooked, the hurting. They are the least, the lost, and the lonely. If you insist on going for the big thing, you will be slow in getting started, if you ever get started at all. But if you are willing to start small, there's no telling what great things can be accomplished.

The poor and the rich are fired up by the same spark

Needy people believe that if they could just accumulate enough money they wouldn't have any problems. Those who are well-off financially believe that if they were less rich their lives would be simpler and happier. They're both partly right and partly wrong. It's not our financial standing that makes the difference in our lives. It's the way we see ourselves and others. It's giving others the freedom to be themselves without judgment.

Spreading the fire brings great healing to my heart

Every time I serve the needy, some measure of healing comes to my heart. It's impossible to spread the fire and not be touched by the power of that fire oneself!

The needy have taught me to be kind—to everyone

I have always found it easier to be kind to strangers than to be patient and kind to those closest to me—my wife, my family, my friends, my co-workers. Strangers I can love because they haven't exhausted my patience yet. But it's a challenge to be kind to those I already know.

I'm convinced that I will be held accountable for the way I treat everyone. I mean everyone. Scary thought. But the needy are my kindness mentors. They have shown me what it's like to be patient. I find it easier now to share the patience I learned from them with those I know and love well.

I know what I want to do with my life

I find great joy in giving away the fire of hope for a better future. It's similar to the perennial role Jimmy Stewart seemed to play in his movies (at least his non-Hitchcock ones!). He was the guy who loved to make others successful. Think of George Bailey in *It's a Wonderful Life*. Think of Elwood P. Dowd in *Harvey* and Jefferson Smith in *Mr. Smith Goes to Washington*. I call it the "spirit of Jimmy Stewart." To make others successful—I think that is what God has in mind for all us.

I want to be like Jimmy Stewart in *It's a Wonderful Life*—bringing freedom from the tyranny of Mr. Potter—by giving the needy economic opportunity and improving their place in life. I like being a pastor, but pastoring isn't the big deal in life. The big deal is bringing freedom to human hearts.

> "In this world, you have to be oh-so-smart or oh-so-pleasant. For years I was smart. I recommend pleasant."
>
> —Harvey the Rabbit in *Harvey*

Jump and the net will appear

Every once in a while, it's great and healthy to take a big risk. In beginning to minister to the needy, one can't dabble. There is always a jump involved. So don't be too squeamish about your results or take your early ventures too seriously. Just jump!

HOW TO START FIRES WITHOUT MATCHES (COME JOIN IN THE EXPERIMENT)

1. Pray a dangerous prayer

My prayer was, "God, I'll take the next open door that comes my way." This is not the sort of prayer that a reasonable person prays.

Step out, and take a risk.

2. Give outreach enough time for the process of change to begin in your heart

Many people miss the blessing that comes to those who do outreach because they give up trying to minister to the needy far too quickly. You can do the right thing with too little resolve and not reap any of the fruitful outcome.

3. Pray that things will get out of control—in the best sense of the word!

As God opens the doors for you, walk through them. Take the risks as they become available. Don't worry about having all the details in advance.

God is in the business of spreading fire. In a sense, things getting out of control is a good thing. When the kingdom of God shows up in its fullness, fires are kindled. Hearts are set ablaze. Minds never think the same again.

ENDNOTES

1. I didn't make that story known publicly to my church. After several years, however, word got back to a businessman in the church who, by himself, paid off the credit-card balance.

2. John Marks, "Burning Man Meets Capitalism," US News & World Report (28 July, 1997), 46.

ABOUT THE AUTHOR

Doug Roe is the senior pastor of The Vineyard, a rapidly growing, outward-focused church in the suburbs of Dayton, Ohio. He launched this church with a handful of people ten years ago while he worked at a grocery store to make ends meet. The church grew as people touched "the least, the lost and the lonely" through many creative means of outreach. The Vineyard now has more than two thousand attendees each weekend. Doug and his wife, Marcie, have four grown sons and two grandchildren.

A QUESTION OF BEING

Worship That Reaches Beyond Church Walls

BY
SALLY
MORGENTHALER

here is an old saying: An acorn never falls far from the tree. This expression is usually applied to parenting, but if one thinks of public worship as the progeny of a congregation, the acorn message as applied to church gatherings might translate into something like this: *A worship service rarely expresses more spiritual, relational, and theological health than its community of faith.*

In recent years, the worship service has been viewed as the front door, the required portal for those who are dechurched or never-churched. The thinking was logical: Do whatever it takes to produce a service that will "knock their socks off." Make sure visitors realize (and realize quickly), "This ain't my grandma's church." Whatever image newcomers had of religion as old, dull, and irrelevant needed to be replaced with one that was upbeat, dynamic, and immediately applicable.

One of the problems with this approach, however, is that it is entirely possible to craft technically sophisticated services without a corresponding sophistication (read here, maturity) of community. We can spend a great deal of time, energy, and resources on a façade, like the false-front town of the Hollywood western, while leaving the interior a tangle of two-by-fours and rusty nails.

We fool no one but ourselves. Worship witnesses whether we want it to or not. The words we use when we gather certainly speak and are a part of that witness, but louder still is the communication that travels beneath the radar—impressions conveyed via actions and omitted actions, tone, body language, and aesthetics. In a world that has moved from the didactic to the experiential, from abstract to lived, visitors take away not so much what has been verbalized as what is intuited, often in spite of our best intentions.

If we want to be outward-focused with our worship in this increasingly skeptical but attentive landscape, we must understand that outsiders' perceptions have not yet been dulled by our self-propaganda. They haven't been taught that, when they sit in the pew Sunday after Sunday, they're supposed to ignore the blatant contradictions between what we as a community of faith do and what we say. They haven't yet figured out how to put a benevolent scrim over hypocrisy. Rather, they will spot what is real and what is not. And make no mistake, they will know (most often, beyond their ability to verbalize) what our connection to God truly entails: occasional deity to Sunday Christian, concept to student, judge to convict, or lover to loved. They will grasp quickly whether our God is "prime mover" or "the one pri-marily moved" by our narcissistic whims. They will perceive whether we who sit there week after week are seeking fun-damental, deep transformation or a way to streamline the next week of our lives. They will ascertain whether the sal-vation we profess is truly a gift or a reward for religious and moral performance. The list could go on.

Yes, worship witnesses, because, among other things, worship is a lived statement of faith. It is one of the key moments when our theology takes on a concentrated, observable form. So, we must ask, just what is it about God and about ourselves that we are expressing when we gather together in the name of Jesus Christ? Is it what we meant to express? Is it what is true, and by virtue of that truth, redemp-tive, freeing, and, above all, pleasing to God? And if it is true that a worship service rarely expresses more spiritual, rela-tional, and theological health than its community of faith, who indeed *are* we as the body of Christ, day in, day out? Have we made worship not just the central thing but, in effect, the only thing?

These are questions of being, questions harder by far to answer than those of doing. They are questions that require us to struggle with the essence of our corporate and indi-vidual identities, questions whose answers don't fit neatly into three-ring notebooks. But since being invariably informs doing, they are the most crucial questions if we truly desire to be people of mission instead of maintenance— *lovers of God and lovers of those God loves.*

BE THE CHURCH OUTSIDE WORSHIP

If we take the Great Commission seriously—"Therefore

go and make disciples of all nations, baptizing them in the name of the Father and of the Son and of the Holy Spirit, and teaching them to obey everything I have commanded you" (Matthew 28:19-20)—*every* aspect of a congregation's life should contain an outward-focused dimension. In that sense, worship is part of an entire matrix of outreach and, as such, should never be expected to carry the entire burden, or even the lion's share, of evangelism. The unchurched are increasingly suspicious of buildings and institutions, a reality that calls into serious question our continued event fixation. When we put all of our eggs into the "big production basket," we become a subcultural curiosity, at best. At worst, we are grossly out of step with how North Americans access the sacred in their everyday lives.

Still, old patterns die hard. What was fresh and effective twenty-five years ago can easily become fossilized as "The way we've always done it." Millions of costly, come-to-our-production mailers go out each year to community residents. While a few recipients do come to our services this way and may even have life-changing experiences as a result, there are countless others who trash these expensive pieces in the nearest circular file.

Those countless others are secretly waiting for an angel with an epidermis to show up. They're waiting for someone who will laugh, hoist a couch, give them places to sleep when their spouses kick them out, find a dentist, listen to their questions, buffet their anger, cry with them in emergency rooms, go to the movies with them, or just commune over cold hot-dogs when the power shuts down. *In this post-Christian dispersion, our front doors are more likely to be carved out of cluttered living rooms, grocery lines, prison lobbies, and bar stools than three thousand dollars worth of steel and glass.*

BE THE CHURCH AT WORSHIP

Having said that, the potential of worship's witness remains. Scripture is amazingly clear that the corporate honor of God was always meant to witness and will continue to do so if we will only let it. (See Psalm 40:3; 57:9; Acts 2:1-12; Acts 2:42-47; Acts 16:25-34; and 1 Corinthians 14: 23-25.) In light of these passages, the challenge for those of us who cut our teeth on '80s event dogma is to actually allow ourselves to be the church at worship. We are so used to trying to do everything on a Sunday morning *but* worship that we may not even know what worship is anymore— what it should contain or what it is that worshipers actually do when they come together.

Fortunately, we don't have to reinvent the wheel or go back to seminary to educate ourselves on worship basics. A number of dedicated individuals have devoted much of their lives to studying Christian worship through twenty centuries. (You will find references to these works at the end of this chapter.) As I have read their works over the years, I've noticed some common themes:

• Worship is our expected, "creaturely" response to the surpassing nature and works of God, the creator. Simply put, worship entails *revelation* (who God is and what God has done/is doing) and *response*. (See Psalm 96:4, 8 and Romans 1:21-25.)

• Worship is *intentional, active adoration of the only one worthy of that adoration.* It is not primarily Christian communication, entertainment, or self-expression, although it may well include aspects of each. (See Psalms 95 and 96.)

• Worship is *God-initiated and God-enabled.* It is not us performing for God or working our way into his presence but God gifting us with his presence and drawing us into active relationship with him solely through Jesus Christ. (See John 6:44; Hebrews 10:19-23; Philippians 3:3.)

- Christian worship is solidly Trinitarian: *the adoration of the Father through the Son by the power of the Holy Spirit.* (See Ephesians 2:18.)
- In worship, *we encounter the living Christ* not just a memorial to Christ. (See Matthew 18:20; Matthew 28:20; and Revelation 1:17-18.)
- Christian worship is *embedded in and experienced primarily through narrative, not through principles or religious ideas* (although the latter may be involved peripherally). In Christian worship, we retell and re-enact the stories of God and God's people in light of *The Story*—God's broad, redemptive work for all of humanity in Jesus Christ. (See Exodus 15:1-21; 1 Chronicles 16; Luke 24:27; Acts 2; and Acts 10:34-43.)
- Worship is a *whole-person activity.* It engages the entire body and all the senses in response to God. (See Psalm 95:6 and Psalm 150.)
- *There is no formula or single expression of worship presented in the New Testament or writings of the church fathers.* However, there is a fairly consistent commonality of elements. These include:

> prayer (including praise, supplication, intercession, thanksgiving, confession, repentance, and commitment)
> song (both composed and spontaneous)
> fellowship (gathering in Christ's name and interceding for and serving one another's needs)
> creeds and faith confessions (the church's deepest convictions)
> Scripture (read, told, and/or preached and carefully interpreted in light of the risen Messiah)
> baptism
> Lord's Supper

BE IN THE CHURCH IN ATTENDANCE

If we raise our hands when the world takes attendance in this new millennium (that is, if we don't just read about unchurched people but are actually in relationship with unchurched people), we cannot help but have our assumptions challenged, specifically those well-worn contentions about how the irreligious view matters of ultimate significance. What seems clear is that an increasing number of North Americans are giving up on the human experiment (otherwise known as the Enlightenment), a project that has had a three-hundred-and-some-year run. The reality is, many of us no longer look to science and the Homo-sapien powers of reasoning to create a better world. After two world wars, Vietnam, the Gulf War, Challenger, Los Angeles riots, the Oklahoma City bombing, the Columbine shootings, the World Trade Center attack, and contested presidential elections, cynicism abounds. And rightly so. We as a race seem to have run out of solutions to our problems. Worse, the solutions themselves have become problems. Just say the words *chad* and *genetic engineering*, and see what reaction you get.

In the sixties, God was dead. In the new millennium, humanism is dead, and as yet, nothing is replacing it. There is, however, a curiously unified chorus crying out for a new set of lenses through which to see this chaotic, fractured world we call home. Some would say this new-millennial chorus is limited to those under thirty-five. Think again. In reality, the post-humanistic choir is a morphing, multi-aged ensemble that, to marketing gurus' chagrin, increasingly defies both demography and psychography. And its post-humanist anthem? Here are some of the highlights:

The supernatural is a given.

Human beings are not enough; we are not the apex of existence.

Relationship—not reason—gives meaning. Connectivity is reality.

For those in our culture who are waxing intentional in their spirituality (and their number is legion), the labels for these new lenses might read like this:

"There is a God, and we are not it."

"We are all a mess."

"We need each other if we're going to get through this mess."

What a long way these new lenses are from the agnosticism, image-orientation, and rugged self-reliance of the '80s. What a long way from what was cutting edge just a decade ago. The implications for worship are staggering. If you and your congregation are truly going to be "in attendance" in your community, if you're going to be an outward-focused congregation in corporate worship, if you're going to truly see through the eyes—the lenses—of people in your communities, you'll need a more radical worship relevance than six happy praise and worship songs, announcements, special music, and a three-point, how-to message with a mesmerizing video clip. Here's what the new lenses require worship, post-masters-of-the-universe, to do.

- ***Turn up the reverence factor.***

    God may be "with us," but God is also "bigger than" and "other." Immanence meets transcendence.

    —much more prayer of all kinds

    —times of silence and meditation

    —worship space that emphasizes height and vertical lines

    —pre-1600 and tribal (from all parts of the globe) Christian art forms

    —fresh rituals to mark the moments

- **_Give people more opportunities for vulnerability._**

  It's OK to not be OK.
  - —corporate confessions
  - —songs and prayers of lament
  - —one-on-one and/or small group intercession
  - —more stories, songs, and art that speak to the reality of struggle
  - —narrative messages with application through community narrative instead of sterile take-home points on an outline

- **_Shift the emphasis from_ I _to_ we.**

  Worship is not a privatized spiritual activity. Worship is the ultimate expression of the body of Christ.
  - —freshly written corporate readings and responses
  - —"we" songs
  - —emphasis on people telling their stories to one another
  - —indigenous worship music, visual art, poetry and prose (from both the congregation and the surrounding community)
  - —worship planning in community for community (see below)

BE THE CHURCH COLLABORATIVE

It takes a community to create worship for a community—especially, a community that wants to be outward-focused. In this era of multiple learning styles and eclectic tastes, worship that has the highest impact is the work of many hands, the vision of many eyes, and melodies playing in many hearts. It has gone through a diverse filter of theological, aesthetic, and logistical perspectives. It has stood the test of numerous "devil's advocate" conversations; its creative energy has been sharpened with the pragmatician's rasp.

Yet many of us as worship leaders and planners are still in Lone-Ranger mode, working as we have for the past decade or two with stacks of songbooks, hymnals, anthems, and CDs on our desk and a cup of coffee to keep us from nodding off. If we're lucky, there's a hastily scribbled note from our supervising pastor outlining the themes for the next six weeks—*if* we're lucky. Maybe we don't even get that. Maybe we're that supervising pastor. Not only do we plan the worship by ourselves, we also type the bulletin and crank out the overheads.

How did we get to this isolated place, where worship reflects nothing more than our default and paucity of imagination, Sunday after Sunday? How did we get to where worship planning is more about filling in prefabricated slots than a creative, collaborative work of art, drawing from the deep well of gifts God has given to our community of faith?

If we are to turn this inward, worship-numbing course around, we must first affirm the sovereignty of God in calling us to *this* community and no other. We must embrace our ministry context with all its inherent limitations and challenges. Until we do, we cannot even begin to think about creating worship in community. Those around us will know instinctively that we have been sitting in our cubicles wishing we had the people, the gifts, and the resources of either the big church down the street or the one that hosted the worship conference we've been raving so much about.

Thus the best preparation for planning worship in community is, first and foremost, an act of submission—to God and God's wisdom, to the uniqueness of our calling, and to the unrepeatable work of God in our midst. In essence, we give our congregations the gift that catalyzes and drives everything else we do as a worshipping body: the gift of particularity. We may be in a suburb of tract houses where the paint choices are down to two. We may be in a small town where everyone looks the same. All the more reason to dig deeper, to get under the apparent sameness, and uncover the rich tapestry below.

To "emboss" the particular work of God in your midst, get out of your cubicle and into weekly, community worship-planning gatherings. Go to one another's living rooms or to a friendly, local café. Get out from under the fluorescent, corporate lighting and outside the gray box.

Expect to be surprised when you do. Because, more often than not, you will witness self-reliant, reclusive pastors; long-dormant visual artists; digital designers who rarely see the light of day; closet musicians; poets; and yes—worship leaders—craft services that no one else has ever imagined, much less seen. Here is where strangers will become a body within the body, caring for one another and maturing around a re-found Levitical task. And here is where a motley, unlikely crew will speak a collective, collaborative, concrete "yes"— week after week—to the question both churched and unchurched are asking: "Can we experience God in your worship service this Sunday (or Friday, or Saturday)?"

Oh, and expect one more thing: evangelism. Your motley crew of artists and imaginers have out-of-the-box, irreligious friends who can be invited into the process of re-imagining sacred experiences. How true it is: No one comes to God unless God draws them (see John 6:44). If you create a living community of worship facilitators, a community where the process is more important than product, where the journey is more important than the performance, and where collaboration is the rule, not the exception, expect to be visited before Sunday morning. Expect the unchurched to arrive at your little café gathering, toolboxes in hand, ready to contribute, ready to build, ready to find the God they seek in your midst. Worship planning, like worship, is a question of being. Expect the unexpected.

References

Emily R. Brink, editor, *Authentic Worship in a Changing Culture* (Grand Rapids, MI: CRC Publications, 1997).

Ralph P. Martin, *Worship in the Early Church* (Grand Rapids, MI: William B. Eerdmans Publishing Co., 1974).

Frank C. Senn, *Christian Liturgy: Catholic and Evangelical* (Minneapolis: Augsburg Fortress Publications, 1997).

James B. Torrance, *Worship, Community and the Triune God of Grace* (Downers Grove, IL: InterVarsity Press, 1996).

Robert E. Webber, *Worship Old and New* (Grand Rapids, MI: Zondervan Publishing House, 1982).

James F. White, *Introduction to Christian Worship* (Nashville: Abingdon, 1980).

About the Author:

Sally Morgenthaler is a native of Colorado. She is, in her own words, "an artist trying to justify having a left brain." As author, photographer, and musician, her unifying passion is the creation and nurture of sacred space. Founder and president of SJM Management Co., Inc., Sally speaks and consults on issues of worship and postmodern culture. She is widely known for numerous articles in leading Christian periodicals and for her insightful book, Worship Evangelism *(Zondervan, 1999). Her children, Peder and Anna Claire, balance her life with billiards and horses, respectively.*

HOOKED ON JESUS

Small Groups That See Beyond Church Walls

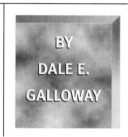

BY DALE E. GALLOWAY

A t age twenty-seven, I was ministering at an old, established church in the Midwest. Everything I proposed, the church people opposed. Even our midweek prayer service was horrible. I was depressed for two days after each of those meetings.

After three or four months of getting nowhere in reaching the town for the Lord, I called my dad to ask for some advice. "I'm dying here," I said. "What should I do?"

Dad talked to me about learning to wait on the Lord. Then he said something amazing: "I'm convinced that any church that will be effective in the days ahead must have small groups."

To this day, I don't know where he got that insight. He was a district superintendent for 140 churches, and not one of them had small groups other than Sunday school classes.

So I went downtown and got acquainted with various business people. Soon enough, six businessmen agreed to be part of a small group, which would meet on Wednesday mornings in a local hotel. I didn't know what to study, so we went through the Gospel of John (see Blackwood's "SMU" Formula, p. 128). When we got to the third chapter where Jesus says, "You must be born again," four of the men had a born-again experience.

On Sunday, some of these men and their families came to church. They did *not* receive a warm welcome. "Who are these folks?" the church people asked me. "What are they doing sitting on my seat?" one lady demanded. Even so, in what I thought to be a dead church, all kinds of small groups began growing around the edges.

From that learn-as-you-go beginning, I made every mistake that can be made in small-group ministry. But I also learned something that changed my life and ministry: Small groups and teams provide the very best way for lay people to get involved in meaningful ministry.

The church in North America still does not understand how to use small groups to reach lost people. We've emphasized fellowship groups, closed groups, covenant groups, accountability groups, and other "us only" groups, but few churches have learned how small groups can become centers of outreach.

> Small groups and teams provide the very best way for lay people to get involved in meaningful ministry.

By contrast, when you look beyond North America, the number-one reason for small groups seems to be to reach unchurched people. According to cell church pioneer Ralph Neighbour, nineteen of the world's twenty largest churches—all of which are on other continents—

have small-group ministries whose primary purpose is evangelism.[1] Using acts of kindness and other ways to demonstrate the love of Christ, they intentionally invite unchurched people into their groups. Since small groups are places where we learn to love one another, they become an ideal venue in which to fulfill the Great Commandment ("love God...love your neighbor") and the Great Commission ("make disciples").

George Gallup, Jr., well-known pollster, has often described how small groups meet the deepest sociological, psychological, and spiritual needs of people. The vital issues in our society today are loneliness, being disconnected, and being uprooted. All these needs are best met when people learn to love one another in a small-group context.

I LOVE SMALL GROUPS

For thirty years now, I've taken part in various "Tender Loving Care" groups. Some of the greatest things that have happened to me personally have occurred in small groups. Some of my best friends in life have come through small groups.

I've also been involved in

The Rhythm Between Small Groups and Large Celebrations

Small cells and corporate worship services are equally important. Groups feed people into weekend worship services, and the big weekend celebrations feed people into small groups.

Why does every church need small groups as a complement to its worship services? Groups

- provide multiple points of entry into the church,

- provide a very effective form of evangelism,

- are the only way to truly care for people,

- accelerate the spiritual growth of individuals and the church, and

- properly shift the work of the church to the people and fulfill Ephesians 4.

building groups in the local church for more than twenty-five years. At New Hope Community Church, we grew from having one group to having more than five thousand people in small groups. At the time I wrote *The Small Group Book*,[2] we were the largest small-group-driven or lay-leader-driven church in North America.

Blackwood's "SMU" Formula for Preaching and Groups

Dr. Jess Moody once shared with me advice he got from Andrew Blackwood, whose books on preaching have influenced tens of thousands of pastors. Dr. Blackwood would come to the Moody home in Florida to go fishing. "What's the secret of great preaching?" Jess asked him on one of those visits. Blackwood's answer was that every good sermon must address these issues:

S—What does the text say?

M—What does it mean?

U—How do you use it?

Every small-group study should cover the same ground.

NEW TESTAMENT WAY OF DOING CHURCH

Small groups represent a rebirth of the New Testament way of doing church. In *Church for the Unchurched*, George G. Hunter III describes what he calls the apostolic congregation. In his research on cutting-edge churches across America, he discovered a rebirth of many of the same characteristics that existed in the early church. He found small-group ministry in every church that effectively reached people and made disciples. He says such congregations "labor to involve everyone, believers and seekers, in small groups."[3]

The church my wife, Margi, and I started followed the very pattern he describes. While the public launch of New Hope is somewhat well-known, many people do not realize that it started with one cell: Our first gathering was a small group that met in a home. One day as I was praying, the Holy Spirit gave me special insight about Acts 20:20. I believe God wanted us to model the implementation of the 20/20 vision described in that passage so we could share this with other churches.

Small groups represent a rebirth of the New Testament way of doing church.

According to eye doctors, anyone with 20/20 vision has clear vision. By analogy, I believe Acts 20:20 contains God's vision for an effective church today. "You know that I have not hesitated to preach anything that would be helpful to you but have taught you publicly and from house to house." Notice the two contexts Paul mentions: "publicly" and "from house to house."

In Jesus' ministry, the home represented a focal point of heart-to-heart fellowship. Jesus frequently went into homes and healed people (see Matthew 8:14-15; 9:23-25; and Mark 1:29-31). He also went into the homes of sinners to draw them into fellowship (see Luke 5:29-32).

Early church history as recorded in the book of Acts clearly shows a focus on the home as a place of significant fellowship and ministry. Some of the very first words about the early church say, "Every day they continued to meet together in the temple courts. They broke bread in their homes and ate together" (Acts 2:46). The Greek word for *house, oikos*, appears at least ninety times in the New Testament, with nine different references to believers worshipping, finding fellowship, or being taught in a house. (See Acts 2:2-4; 2:46; 5:42; 10:24-48; 16:25-34; 16:40; 20:17-20; 21:8-14; 28:30-31.)

The way to build a great church is to follow the master plan that was developed so effectively in the early church.

Meet in the "house of God" on the weekend to celebrate together the resurrection power of Jesus. Then throughout the week, meet house-to-house in small groups for heart-to-heart fellowship.

OUTREACH AND HOPE IN SMALL GROUPS

This New Testament blueprint for building a successful church is in perfect step with meeting the needs of people who are lonely and isolated in the twenty-first century. Small groups present a tremendous opportunity to reach unchurched people by meeting them at their point of need. This plan is perfect for our generation. Our society is coming apart at the seams, and people are desperate for a pathway to healing and connecting. In a society characterized by addictions, family breakdown, isolation, and loneliness, churches need to respond by developing effective small-group ministries.

TWO DECADES OF TESTING AT NEW HOPE

At New Hope Community Church, we created groups targeted to meet people either at their point of need or interest. We sponsored nurturing groups, which we called Tender Loving Care groups. We also encouraged task groups, support and recovery groups, fellowship groups, and special-interest groups. Through these entry points, many people connected to God, to each other, and to our church.

About 90 percent of the members who joined while I was pastor came as new believers. Our experience proves that small groups are an effective way to implement friendship evangelism.

TARGET NEEDS AND INTERESTS

If small groups target people's pain, people will drive any distance for help. I can still see a retired plumber with calloused hands, standing up at one of our leader-training meetings. With tears running down his cheeks, he shared how he had made a commitment to Christ when a friend invited him to a small group. Now he was the leader of a small group, and that very week during the prayer time three new members had committed themselves to follow Jesus.

> If small groups target people's pain, people will drive any distance for help.

A month later, this man's wife of many years died. Sometime after her homegoing, we met in the hallway at church. With tears in his eyes once more, he shared how their grandson had begun attending their small group and had also become a Christian.

In Portland, one of the most unchurched cities in America, New Hope Community Church grew to sixty-four hundred members, most of whom had never belonged to a church before. Many of these people found their entry point into the church through the evangelistic ministry of a small group.

Broken Members, Mended Body by Kathi Mills chronicles the story of several small-group ministries at New Hope and how each conducted outreach by targeting needs and interests. Her summary statement voices my conviction exactly: "Jesus always meets people at their point of need."[4]

CONNECTING PEOPLE

Small groups also form a vital link in assimilation. Long ago, I heard church-growth authority C. Peter Wagner make this statement at a seminar: "If you do not get the people in

> In a small group, every believer becomes a caregiver, and everyone is cared for.

How to Keep Evangelism at the Center of Your Small Group

- **Empty chair**—Keep an open chair at each meeting to represent someone you would like to bring into the group.

- **Prospect list**—Make a list with names of people, both outside and inside the church, who need to be in a group. Think it, ink it, pray it, and work it.

- **Social evening**—Start a new group by having a social evening and inviting all the people on a prospect list. Share the vision of the new group, and invite people to give it a try.

- **Reporting**—Ask group leaders to regularly fill out a short report that highlights how many newcomers they are reaching.

- **Baptisms**—When you baptize new Christians, ask their small-group leaders to stand alongside the pastor as witnesses or to pray for the person being baptized.

- **Lessons**—Be sure that questions that deal with becoming a new Christian are included in the small-group lessons you create or recommend.

- **Acts of kindness**—Encourage people to put their caring into action. Have small acts of kindness earn the right to invite people to a friendship group.

- **Reproduction**—Build the idea of reproduction into the DNA of each group by putting an apprentice in place when you start a group. Let everyone know that either the leader or the apprentice is preparing to start another group.

- **Leadership training**—In regular training, explain to leaders how to present the message of salvation and how to follow up with someone who has just made a faith commitment to Christ.

- **New groups**—Continually create new groups that target needs and interests.

your church connected within the first two years, you will lose them out the back door." His statement proved to be true in my own pastoral ministry at that time. A few years later, I found the time window to be shortened to one year, then six months, then three months. Now it's more like two or three weeks.

How does a church get people connected with each other? You get them into a small group. How do you close the back door? You get them into small groups. Small groups are the best places for the making of disciples.

Small groups are also places for effective pastoral care. In small groups, not only do people connect with the leader or apprentice leaders who care for them, but pastoral care is multiplied because ten people end up caring for ten people. In fact, I know of no more effective way to provide care for people today than through small group ministry. In a small group, every believer becomes a caregiver, and everyone is cared for.

Other Pacesetting Churches Around the World

New Hope is not the only church to discover the power of outreach through small groups. At a seminar I led, one of the participants made this fascinating comment: "In the '60s, we would intentionally get someone into the drug culture by bringing them to a small group. We'd meet at a home, sit in a relaxed atmosphere, make newcomers feel comfortable, and pass a joint, and they'd get hooked. Ever since I became a Christian, I've wondered why the church doesn't use small groups to evangelize and reach people."

> Small groups are places to learn to love Jesus' way.

If groups can be used to bring people into addiction to drugs, think of the power to "hook" people on the love of Jesus. Small groups are places to learn to love Jesus' way.

George Hunter devoted almost 25 percent of his book *Church for the Unchurched* to the role of small groups in reaching the unchurched. *Sharing the Journey*, Robert Wuthnow's landmark three-year study of small groups in

America, concluded that some 55 percent of group members report that small-group involvement enabled them to share their faith.[5] Carl George, author of *Nine Keys to Effective Small-Group Leadership*, regularly polls people at training events. He consistently finds that one out of four groups across North America report at least one new faith commitment during the previous twelve months.[6]

HOW TO CREATE A VICTORY CIRCLE

Several years ago, in conjunction with my role on the board of directors for his Church Growth International, I joined a group of other pastors for breakfast with Paul Yonggi Cho in Korea. Someone asked, "Where do you find leaders for the twenty-five thousand small groups you have?" Dr. Cho's immediate reply was, "I get them from new Christians."

Obviously he doesn't say, "OK, you've found Christ yesterday. Now, today you're the leader of this group." Instead leaders work with the new Christians, discipling them, bringing them along, and giving them responsibility step by step. In this way, the leaders create a continual supply of new leaders.

Multiplication will always come through the starting of new groups because groups are forced to expand their circle, build prospect lists, find more people, and fill open chairs by inviting others. Healthy groups can reproduce, on average, every five to six months. Some will need only four months, while others will need twelve or more.

> **Multiplication will always come through the starting of new groups.**

A successful small-group system reaches new people, disciples believers, helps people grow in their love for God and each other, develops leaders, and creates a strong congregation.

START WITH A TOTALLY INTEGRATED APPROACH

Today we see a lot of churches "with" small groups but only a few churches "made up of" small groups. To get the best out of your groups, you need to determine how to get what you're after. A lot of good can grow out of healthy groups. To get the best results, small groups cannot be just an afterthought; they must serve as the circulatory system of the entire church.

Karen Hurston has identified three ways churches can approach small-group ministry. I recommend the third option if you want to develop a strong, thriving small-group ministry.

Appendage System — In some churches, a handful of lay people lead the charge for small groups. They have taken initiative to start or maintain groups. They love small groups and are faithful in championing them, even with little support or ongoing training. But because small groups are not central to the church's vision or to the pastor's heart, they are at best an "appendage" to the entire church body.

Departmentalized System — "Do you know where we can find a small-group pastor to head up our groups?" That question signals a dangerous situation. Small groups will never rise any higher than the senior pastor's commitment and heart toward small groups. The senior pastor can recruit help, but if the senior pastor hands off groups entirely, small groups will be just one more "department" in the church.

> To get the best results, small groups cannot be just an afterthought; they must serve as the circulatory system of the entire church.

Totally Integrated System — At New Hope Community Church, all the people we brought on staff had responsibility to recruit, to equip, and to train leaders for small groups in their area or areas. Every aspect of the church structure was organized around the small groups. We also required every pastor's personal involvement in a small group.

For example, at one point our children's ministry was primarily limited to Sunday school. Then we brought on someone who caught the vision for "totally integrated" groups. Over five years, she created all kinds of additional lay pastor opportunities for working with children. She oversaw the launch of kids' clubs, scouting, choirs, and even a group for children from dysfunctional families. She had sixteen different ways children could be in small groups. We eventually had sixteen hundred children meeting in small groups, with something available every day of the week—in addition to a fine small-group-based Sunday school program.

CREATE A SYSTEM THAT PRODUCES MULTIPLICATION AND OUTREACH

Envision people leading others to Christ, discipling people, caring for people, praying for the sick, sharing life with one another, and building up the body of Christ; most of this can best take place through the building of community groups. Successful small-group systems always seem to share seven key actions.

> Build leaders, and they will build groups.

Here are seven key actions for a successful small-group system that is continually multiplying, giving care, bringing people to Christ, making disciples, and developing new leaders:

Key action 1: Develop leaders

Build leaders, and they will build groups. The most important job of the pastoral staff is to build lay leaders who will build small groups. Don't be afraid to ask for that level of commitment.

Make sure every group has an apprentice in place.

Many churches, including New Hope, build groups from a leadership nucleus that contains different roles: the leader, the assistant or apprentice leader, and the host/hostess. The leader might lead the lesson, while the assistant makes some of the necessary phone calls and the host takes responsibility for lining up a meeting place and refreshments. Over time, the assistant or apprentice does everything the leader does. To prepare enough leaders for the future, make sure every group has an apprentice in place.

The Holy Spirit gives each church the gifts it needs for effective ministry. In many churches, potential leaders are present but not full-grown. They're undeveloped, and you need to help them grow up. Show them what to do, have them do it, and then use the experience as a teaching point. Then show them the next step, have them do it, and debrief together. Any time I did anything in pastoral ministry, I'd take along one of these potential leaders. As we traveled to the ministry location and back, we'd talk about it. This method follows Jesus' example; he took these same steps as he trained leaders!

If you want to have a dynamic small-group ministry, you'll need to have a "staircase" full of leaders, each at a different point, and each moving forward one step at a time. You multiply yourself and your ministry as you develop new leaders.

Focusing on developing leaders will build the multiplication DNA into the very core of your small-group ministry.

Key action 2: Provide advancement opportunities

One weakness of many churches is that lay people have no opportunity to advance in ministry. New Hope had three

> You multiply yourself and your ministry as you develop new leaders.

different advancement steps for lay pastors in small-group ministry. At the beginning level, called *lay pastor in training*, the person is an apprentice. The apprentices had a Thursday-to-Saturday kick-off event called a Super Bowl. Then about one hundred days later, we publicly dedicated each apprentice to become a *lay pastor*. The lay pastor would attend regular training and lead a group. Over time, a lay pastor could move to a third level, called *lay pastor leader*. Not only did lay pastor leaders lead their own groups, but they also accepted responsibility for three to five other leaders, as well as for receiving further ministry training.

Using this advancement system, you can provide a lot of ministry without hiring any staff. It differs from a business model in that the leaders remain involved in a group. They model while they teach. I pastored a large church, and I still led a group. I needed the group myself, and I still needed to be producing new leaders.

Movement up the ladder didn't need to stop at the *lay pastor leader* step, however. Half the paid pastoral staff at New Hope emerged this way; they started in a small group. At New Hope, small groups provide the primary place for training.

Key action 3: Train

Can you make the offer, "You supply the person, and we'll supply the training"? Every church needs a system for training its leaders thoroughly. Some churches over-train, and their lay leaders never get to do actual ministry. Other churches under-train, throwing people into ministry without preparation or support. At New Hope, we tried to make every training opportunity count. We developed four primary ways to keep training balanced and at the forefront:

(1) Our *initial* training occurs at the previously mentioned Super Bowl event, which we eventually offered three times a year.

(2) We hold *regular* training at times our people find to be convenient: during Sunday school or over a Wednesday-evening supper, for example. We go over a lesson that they could guide their small group through. In the process, we also model what we want our groups to be and do. We do this training weekly; some churches train once or twice a month.

(3) Training also occurs *on-the-job* as people take part in groups and lead them.

(4) Finally, we provide continual *skill* training for as long as someone leads a group. Many of our most popular resources have come out of those advanced training times, including the kit *Ministry Skills for Small Group Leaders* (available from 20/20 Vision at 1-800-420-2048). Other examples of specialty, ongoing training include Carl George's book, *Nine Keys to Effective Small Group Leadership* and its corresponding *Nine Facets* video series.

Key action 4: Supervise

Most of all, Christian leaders need encouragement. How many pastors almost quit every Monday? I sure did. If I needed that kind of encouragement, how much more do lay leaders!

The main objective of lay pastor leaders' and staff pastors' visits to each group (ideally, every seven to eight weeks and by appointment), is to provide encouragement and support. Beyond that, we tried to cover the following checklist:

- ☐ See if the leadership team is in place and functioning healthily.
- ☐ Review the prospect list of potential group members to see if it is being talked and prayed about. Ask for the names of target families.

☐ Check progress toward the goal of one family added to membership every six months.

☐ Help identify potential lay pastor trainees.

☐ Observe whether the leaders are using various principles of successful groups.

Each time we made such a visit, group quality would rise. On-the-job supervision will multiply the effectiveness of your small groups!

Key action 5: Hold leaders accountable

How do you build an appropriate, workable level of accountability into your small group ministry? A surprising number of churches have no reporting loop. If you don't require your group leaders to attend training, you're not going to get very much from them. In addition to requiring that they commit to training, ask for regular reports. This may be a simple sheet that they fill out, or it might be something the lay pastor leader fills out when interviewing and coaching each lay pastor. By requiring team accountability, you weed out people who want to do their own thing, and you can prevent difficulties down the road.

Key action 6: Recruit

Remember that public announcements rarely draw out the leaders you need. Quality people usually don't step forward in response to general announcements. Instead, they'll come forward after someone spends time with them and recruits them one-on-one. Jesus did it this way, and it's the way that works best in most places.

I remember receiving an invitation from the CEO of a large company in Portland to have breakfast together. I wanted to meet him, so I agreed. We had barely ordered when he started recruiting me to serve on the Portland Boy Scouts Council. Though I had received many such requests in the mail and had tossed them all unanswered, I said yes to this man. Why? He recruited me one-on-one.

The best recruiting happens one by one.

He never would have gotten me to agree if he hadn't shared face to face his own vision and excitement about how worthwhile it was. The best recruiting happens one by one.

Key action 7: Sponsor events

Healthy churches are often very busy places. With so many programs going on, how can you make small groups a core value? We did this by having regular major events, such as our three-day Super Bowl. Not only does the event provide great benefit itself, but the buildup beforehand also makes a strong impact. Our pre-Super Bowl promotion included people's stories and various creative momentum builders. This strategy put small groups at center stage.

During the Super Bowl, we cheered on the new trainees, we shared victory stories, and we cast overall vision for why small groups are needed. Then we mapped out all the particulars including:

- a vision of how small groups can reach people
- the role of the Holy Spirit and prayer for the spiritual ministry of groups
- how to develop a personal testimony (As you love people, you'll have opportunities to share your faith.)
- role descriptions for various leadership opportunities
- training in how to place a phone call to someone you don't know
- principles of how to have a successful small group

PRAYER AND THE HOLY SPIRIT

Every effective small-group ministry I've seen across the world emphasizes prayer and the Holy Spirit. It's important that your leaders be filled with the Holy Spirit, that they have fellowship with the Holy Spirit in their prayer lives, and that they obey the Holy Spirit. That's what gives any ministry power and spiritual effectiveness.

After that starting point, you need a system in place to get the result you're after. The best way you can spend time in ministry is helping a small group leader grow. Small groups have the ability to break out of every human limitation you face. Buildings do not limit them because groups use people's homes, restaurants, and offices. They can meet anytime and anywhere that works for the group members. In short, you face only one limit: leadership. Have you learned what it means to be a leader-maker? Do you have a system in place to take your lay leadership to a whole new level of effectiveness?

To multiply small groups in your church and help them be effective, you need to develop the right system. As you think about what fits you, think about how you can maximize small group ministries to fulfill the desired purposes and to benefit the most people, especially those who do not yet have a relationship with Jesus Christ.

Most church leaders make small groups too complicated. Successful leaders see it big and keep it simple. They learn to focus on what is really important, and to keep their focus there.

See it big and keep it simple.

Small Group Ministry Scorecard

What do you have in place? Where do you need to improve?

In place	Need to improve	
☐	☐	**1.** Leadership development
☐	☐	**2.** Advancement opportunities
☐	☐	**3.** Training
☐	☐	**4.** Supervision
☐	☐	**5.** Accountability
☐	☐	**6.** Recruiting
☐	☐	**7.** Sponsoring events

Implementing Outward-Focused Small Groups in a Traditional Church

1. Do share your vision with key leaders who are the influencers.

2. Do not forget your church has its history and traditions.

3. Do take inventory of the groups, resources, and opportunities you already have.

4. Do know your own people's needs, interests, and backgrounds.

5. Do map out where you want to be five years from now in small group ministry.

6. Break your master plan into manageable steps.

7. Write down what you are going to do in the next three months to go to the next level of small-group growth in your church.

8. Do practice this wise principle: Don't threaten but expand.

9. Do begin with a model group or groups.

10. Do take time to make the change gradually.

11. Do build some flexibility into your small group system.

12. Do win people by caring.

13. Do gradually change your staff into people who will build their ministries using small groups.

14. Do give priority to prayer and the person of the Holy Spirit.

ENDNOTES

1. Ralph W. Neighbour, Jr., *Where Do We Go From Here?* (Houston: Touch Publications, 2000), 37.

2. Dale E. Galloway and Kathi Mills, *The Small Group Book*, (Grand Rapids, MI: Fleming H. Revell, 1995).

3. George G. Hunter III, *Church for the Unchurched* (Nashville: Abingdon Press, 1996), 32.

4. Kathi Mills, *Broken Members, Mended Body* (Ventura, CA: Regal Books, 1988), 72.

5. Robert Wuthnow, *Sharing the Journey* (New York: The Free Press, 1994).

6. Carl George, *Nine Keys to Effective Small-Group Leadership* (Mansfield, PA: Kingdom Publishing, 1997), 6.

ABOUT THE AUTHOR

Dr. Dale Galloway began preaching a message of hope from atop the snack shack at a drive-in theater in Portland, Oregon. This unorthodox approach to church planting in 1972 led to the growth and development of New Hope Community Church. During his 23 years as pastor, Dr. Galloway nurtured the congregation to an average Sunday attendance of more the six thousand.

Dr. Galloway is a pioneer in developing need-meeting ministries led by lay people. He has conducted conferences in every major city across the United States. Pastors from all over the world came to New Hope's Church Growth Institute to learn how to create and sustain effective cell-group ministries. By the time Dr. Galloway left New Hope in 1995, there were five hundred lay pastors ministering to the church's five-thousand-plus small-group members.

Dr. Galloway now serves as dean of the Beeson International Center for Biblical Preaching and Church Leadership. He is the author or editor of nineteen books, including Leading With Vision *and* Making Church Relevant.

Dr. Galloway and his wife, Margi, have two children.

CREATING A PLACE TO LAND

Youth Ministry Beyond Church Walls

BY
DAN
SLATTER

y life story hinges on accidentally stumbling into contact with a church through a friend. I only became interested in church when I had a friend to go with and the prospect of meeting some more people my age. Also, being a healthy teenage lad, I really fancied one of the girls!

Somehow I managed to find faith and then cling to it through the friends that I made and some grace-filled youth leaders. I gave my life to God because I saw something in my newfound friends in the youth group that I liked and wanted for my life. Not being the sharpest tool in the box, I took awhile to make the connection between what they were like and their relationship with the living God.

OUR TASK

The most important task at hand is to live out the Great Commission: Go and make disciples of all people, young and old. How do we do this among this generation of young people? How do we see these young people—whose lives would normally never cross paths with church or Christians—come to meet Christ? Does church need to change in order to stay the same? The church is hemorrhaging young people; how do we stop the loss and dare to look to grow?

We call our church Warehouse. We've learned two important principles that are now part of the DNA of Warehouse and will continue to stimulate growth among young people. These principles will release our young people to be all that God desires them to be and bring totally unchurched young people into our church families to find Christ.

A first step must be to get our head around today's society and western culture. The church must adapt to not only survive but also fulfill the Great Commission. Jesus met people where they were at in life, on their turf. The first golden principle is that we need to present Jesus and his bride, the church, in a culturally relevant way and establish a strong cultural presence.

CULTURE SHIFT

The society we live in is constantly changing. Most observers of culture would agree that there has been massive change in recent times. Leonard Sweet helpfully explains the shift in culture over the past few decades and into this new millennium by using the metaphor of "natives and immigrants." He suggests that people born after 1962 are natives in today's society and those born before that are immigrants.[1] This classification implies that we have gone through a major shift in western culture in the past forty years. And western culture is still evolving even now.

I hear people say that young people and youth culture are just the same today as they were thirty years ago but with a few more gadgets. This is simply not true. The current youth generation is arguably the most hurting generation that has ever lived on the face of God's earth. Just look at the statistics about this generation. You'll see more teen suicides, more teen pregnancies, more teen drug users, and more teens from broken homes. Today's youth culture is one that thrives on extremes.

TIME FOR A CHANGE

Taking note of these changes, we must allow for a similar shift in our own thinking. How do we present the gospel to this generation? I would suggest that we need to think outside the box about the way we share the gospel. It is not that we change the *gospel* (Hebrews 13:8), but that the *way* we get it out to this hurting generation and share Jesus must change. Now, I am not disarming the power of the gospel. The gospel is full of power (Romans 1:16). We just want young people to give the gospel airtime in their lives.

In the United Kingdom, the biblical visual image of the wine and wineskin (Luke 5:37) has been helpful. The wine is the same, but we need a new skin to carry it in as the old skin is cracked and leaking. The old way does not do its job in this generation. Technology, stories, and visual stimulation are essential for reaching teenagers today.

I am privileged to be able to speak at assemblies in

some high schools near where I live to share a bit of Jesus. When I return a few weeks later, I ask the young people, "Do you remember what I said or did last time?" They always recall the stories or visuals I used to illustrate my point. As we continue the conversation, they begin to link the story or the video clip to what I said about Jesus.

To be effective in reaching teenagers, we must learn the new cultural language and share God's message in words they can understand. And then we need to be culturally present in order to give it. We would never send missionaries into a country that did not share our mother tongue if they had not first at least started to learn the country's language. Equally, we would not expect them to share Jesus with these people effectively if they were not present in that country.

LANDING PADS

Western culture is a mission field with its own unique cultural features. In working with young people, our challenge is to create simple landing pads for this unchurched generation to land on. We need to make these landing pads as numerous, accessible, and varied as possible.

Some people are gifted in drawing others into church, so we try to release them to do what they do well. At the same time, we build events or ideas around them to help. Luke, one of the students in Warehouse, is really into BMXing. He regularly rides at our local skate park to meet others. He is a great rider, and the other riders respect him for his ability and the fact that he is a top bloke. They are just in the process of making the connection between his being a nice guy and his being a Christian.

Other effective ministries are springing up all around. Some churches run mentoring programs for disaffected young people. We've been involved in running music events that provide a safe environment for young people. A church just north of London has set up skate parks. Another church we work with takes on long-term unemployed young people to give them work experience and equip them with new skills. We must seek to use the resources at our church's disposal to bless our communities and give young people those safe, nonthreatening landing pads.

The runway at Hong Kong International airport is said to be one of the most difficult to land on. There is a serious danger of overshooting it and ending up in the sea, and hills surround the airport and the city. It takes a seasoned pilot to land a big plane on this runway. We see young people who are looking to land in a safe refuge from a harsh world. Their "planes" are big and messed up, carrying tons of baggage. They're confused and spat out by society. But we tend to expect them to land on our narrow church runways. We demand that they emigrate from their culture to our alien one.

We need to create big, fat runways—runways like the ones NASA uses for the space shuttles—so that young people can feel safe enough to even try to land. We need safe, nonthreatening places for young people to come to. Then we can start to build genuine relationships that have real value. We need wide runways so the young people do not feel like they're our latest evangelistic project.

We must expect that, when they land, young people will bring their baggage with them into our churches. Most of the young people who come into our church from totally unchurched backgrounds start by joining socially. We accept them and say that people can "belong before they believe." This acceptance flies in the face of most churches, where young people are expected to come only after they have things sorted out. In other words, they tend to say, "believe, prove it, and then you can belong." Jesus never told the disciples that they had to be perfect citizens and respectful young men to be in his church. If that were what he wanted, he certainly would not have chosen that mix of guys to be his disciples. They did not have respectable religious backgrounds, but a lifelong journey led them into God's throne room.

DIRTY HANDS

I once received a phone call from a well-known Christian organization in the UK about a young man named Matt. This organization does lots of work among people in the prison system. Matt was seventeen years old and in a young offenders institute for a number of convictions, mostly triggered by his alcohol addiction. He found Jesus while serving time for these offenses. The prison chaplain was trying, through this organization, to hook him up with a church near his home city upon release. When I told the woman on the phone that we would love to have Matt as part of our family and would do everything we could to help him adjust to life on the outside, she sounded relieved. You can imagine my shock when she revealed to me that we were the fourth church she had tried. The other churches did not want young people like Matt in their congregations.

After speaking with some other leaders in the church, I realized that offering to take Matt on was a massive commitment that could get very messy and might explode in my face at some point. It also dawned on me that this was the exact person that Jesus would have tried to offer a hand of friendship to. He was an outcast of society just like the criminal crucified alongside Jesus; his last new follower before his death. Hey, we have to get our hands dirty as Jesus did. We must open the doors of our churches to accept these young people and welcome them as they arrive into our lives.

LONG-TERM RELATIONSHIPS

We have to earn the right to speak into these young lives. You may ask: How do I do this? I do it by simply being like Jesus—accepting the young people as they are and being there for the long haul, no matter what. So many things in today's society, where these young people are growing up, are about a cheap, short-term high. We, the church, must be different. Some of our leaders have had to stick in there through overdoses, teenage pregnancy, abortion, violence, self-harm, and drug addiction, to name a few. Whatever life throws at these young people or that they throw at us, we must demonstrate that our friendship will stick and is nonjudgmental.

Friendship and family influences are two of the most important factors in leading new Christians to faith commitments. In today's youth culture, these two influences are as important as ever, if not even more so, as the importance of relationships is a common theme running through this current youth generation. Friendships are the key, as indeed Jesus found with his twelve pals, the disciples.

The second principle we have found for reaching those youth beyond church walls is to equip the young people we already have. We must train a new army of missionaries to reach this generation that is in free-fall, running out of options, and leaping from one short-term high to the next.

The exciting news is that most of God's major

movements on the face of this earth have been initiated by *young* men and women. Perhaps that's because of youthful passion or because we're more flexible in our youth. But what we can definitely say is that God uses young people like the ones in your youth group. If we can harness this resource and effectively disciple these teenagers, God will do the rest.

How many young people do you have contact with outside your church community? Now think about how many young people you have in your group. How many friends who are not Christians does each of the young people in your group have? Probably loads—a whole class for starters, and then there's gym club on a Thursday night and baseball on the weekend. They have literally hundreds of friends. It's when we're teenagers that we have our largest sphere of friends; the sphere shrinks as we get older. Therefore it is just simple multiplication that leads us to realize how essential it is to invest in our church young people, to train them as Jesus did his disciples.

NATURAL LEADERS

Those of you with young children will be able to understand this: If one kindergarten child catches a bad cold, it is only a matter of time until all of the children in the class come down with it. If we can infect our young people with a contagious version of the gospel, that message has the potential to spread far and wide very quickly. We must train our youth and infect them with a contagious dose of Jesus.

To take this theory a step further, I was inspired by an Anthony Hopkins movie, *Instinct.* At one point Ethan Powell is in the hills with the gorillas and is trying to be accepted into their community in order to study them. He soon comes to the realization that he will have to be accepted by Silverback, the dominant group leader, before the rest of the group will trust him. No matter what circle of life we are part of, there are always natural leaders, people whom others will follow no matter what they suggest. Look at what Hitler managed to get ordinary people to do.

One of our young people is one of those natural leaders. Life dealt this guy a bad hand, which led to his being pretty messed up before he started hanging around with some of us from the church. In fact, the first time I met him, he locked himself in a cupboard. The drugs he had pumped into his body over many years of being a hurt young man made him too paranoid to even meet us. But even in those early days, before he made a commitment to follow Christ, there was something about him that magnetically drew people to his messed up life. After he committed his life to Jesus, he organized everything from picnics to walks in the countryside. If I had suggested those things, our young people would have laughed their heads off at me. Somehow he managed to get hordes of young people to go. If we can influence the natural leaders, others will surely follow.

These leaders are often not the young people that we would normally look to as leaders. They tend to be the rebellious, cynical types who are on the fringe of what we do. We need to look beyond the behavior to the heart and God-given call. The chracteristics these young people display are often leadership skills that are warped and need redeeming.

One eighteen-year-old girl who was part of Warehouse was so rebellious it used to drive me mad. I found it a real challenge to see beyond this rebellion often manifesting itself in my face. But a frustrated leader was trapped inside that girl. Slowly but surely, we drew that leader out through perseverance, grace, prayer, and helping her to see the trait in herself. Now God is really using her among her fellow students at the university.

REACHING BEYOND CHURCH WALLS

We must make Jesus real to this generation by being culturally relevant. The church has to scratch young people where they itch. We must get back to the core values of the church: to be there to serve our communities and be a safe place of blessing.

We must be present in today's culture. Too often the church runs scared from culture rather than taking the bull by the horns and redeeming it. We must be a strong presence in today's society. Then we must be prepared for the consequences of this choice: It may well be messy as we try to unconditionally accept these young people.

Finally we must act on the biblical mandate to train and release our young people as missionaries to their own generation. We must equip them and pray for God's grace and protection for them, then release them into their calling while they are full of enthusiasm and energy and with few commitments in life.

ENDNOTE

1. Leonard Sweet, *AquaChurch* (Loveland, CO: Group Publishing, Inc., 1999).

About the Author

Dan Slatter has a burning passion to see God move powerfully amongst this predominately unchurched global generation of young people. Throughout his journey in the practical outworking of faith and ministry, Dan has grappled with the issues raised in this book. He seeks to make the bride of Christ beautiful and attractive to young people and help them engage in a real relationship with Jesus. Dan spends most of his time communicating with young people and leading Warehouse, the youth and student congregation of Revelation Church, which meets in multiple cities south of London, England.

CHURCH REPRODUCTION

New Congregations Beyond Church Walls

BY ROBERT E. LOGAN

Healthy churches grow. Few people would disagree with that statement. Disciples make other disciples, leaders train other leaders, groups give birth to other groups, and ministries plant the seeds of other ministries. This is the natural order and progression of growth. However, many people stop short of recognizing that churches should continue to grow beyond their own walls. They are designed to start other churches.

When Jesus said, "Go and make disciples of all nations," he gave us a mission. Shortly afterward, when the church was born at Pentecost, the Holy Spirit gave us the means to accomplish that mission. The church is God's chosen tool to fulfill the Great Commission. How can it accomplish so large a goal? Only by multiplying itself over the face of the whole earth. One church alone cannot possibly reach the world. One church alone cannot even reach a whole city. Here's the honest truth: To reach more people, we need more churches.

WHO NEEDS MORE CHURCHES?

Some people doubt that additional churches are really needed. They wonder, "Can't people just attend the ones that already exist?" Try this eye-opening exercise. Make a list of all the churches in your area. Find out the seating capacity of each one. Add up the total number of available seats. Double that number, assuming that every congregation is so vitally alive that two services are necessary to hold all the people. Now compare that number to the total population in the area. Is there room in the existing churches to nurture young Christians? As God brings in the harvest, will there be adequate churches to open their doors?

Church planting is the most effective available means of church growth; it's far more effective than simply trying to make existing churches larger. Every individual church is unique, even those within the same denomination that are located near each other. Each has its own style and personality and, because of that uniqueness, is better equipped to reach certain people.

A woman once brought an out-of-town relative who does not know Christ to one of her church services. He really enjoyed the alternative style and atmosphere and said, "If there was a church like this where I live, I'd start going." Churches with different styles are often required to reach different generations, ethnic groups, language groups, and subcultures.

Not only do more churches provide the opportunity for more styles, they are better positioned for effective evangelism. Would you rather have one church of one thousand people or ten churches of one hundred people? Which would reach more people for Christ? Research shows that the smaller churches would evangelize more people by far. One of the most startling discoveries of the research was that small churches—those averaging fifty-one people in attendance—were sixteen times more effective in winning new converts to Christ than megachurches.[1]

An executive working in a service-oriented branch of business also discovered that multiplication is better than addition. Reorganizations had consolidated several branches into larger regional service centers in hopes that work would be processed more efficiently, needs would be met more effectively, and the business would save money. This "bigger is better" mentality backfired completely as production, service, and quality all went down. Additionally, a much higher percentage of the employees began filing grievances, were less satisfied with their jobs, and sought employment elsewhere.

When a church grows so big that its members don't feel personally cared for, people leave. When staff members are frustrated by the pressures of managing too many areas of responsibility and don't receive the affirmation, training, resources, and support needed to accomplish their ministry, they leave. Whether in ministry or in the marketplace, these principles ring true.

LOOKING OUTWARD

If starting more churches is the most effective way to reach others and fulfill the Great Commission, a church that is truly outward-focused will be a church that starts more churches. A church is never on level ground, just coasting along. Although you may not see the changes week by week, it is either moving toward death or moving toward life and growth. Churches with an inward focus are moving inexorably toward death. The outward-focused church, however, has a vision that reaches far beyond itself and out into the surrounding community and the world. It will grow and make a difference for the kingdom.

In London, a low-income housing project surrounds a polluted lake. Just down the street is a wealthy church with a white-collar membership. For years, this church struggled to reach the housing project-community but was unsuccessful because of the huge socioeconomic gap. Finally the church hired an evangelist, Conrad Parsons, who worked half of the time in the church and half of the time in the housing project.

Conrad began building relationships with people in the community and listening to their concerns. One woman spoke for all the people who lived in the low-income housing area when she voiced what was on her heart. Three concerns rang through loud and clear. The number one problem was the polluted lake. Two, she wanted to bring people together within the community. Three, she wanted a better place to raise her children.

Conrad got started. He recruited a team of eighty volunteers to clean up the lake. Forty came from the housing project and forty came from the wealthy church. They worked side by side, poor and rich, cleaning up the lake. One woman in the project said, "It used to be them and us. Now it's just us."

The team got a lot of publicity. Newspapers, radio stations, and television networks all picked up the story, and people were energized. The momentum created by the cleanup effort motivated them to find additional ways to improve their situation.

The residents committee (made up almost entirely of non-Christians) was pleased with the changes in the community and invited the wealthy church to start a worship service in the housing project. Conrad and his team began by teaching the people Christmas carols and stories about Jesus. The excitement caught on and spread throughout the community. Soon the housing-project community had more than a worship service; it had a church. It became known as the Pond Church. Rather than just focusing on reaching individuals, these people are planting the gospel in a whole community.

What a missed opportunity it would have been had the wealthy church not looked out beyond its own walls. Too often churches compete with each other instead of recognizing that they are on the same side. We become territorial, protecting our own turf and trying to squeeze out rivals. If the goal of the church is to spread the gospel and advance the kingdom, reproducing other churches can only help us in reaching this end. We are not meant to compete but to cooperate.

GROWTH FROM THE OUTSIDE IN

Not only does church planting further the goals of God's kingdom, but it revitalizes the churches that participate. Nothing gets a church off the proverbial couch like reaching out. Just as individual believers need to take the focus off themselves and reach out to others in order to grow and be healthy, churches need to look beyond their own congregations and help start others.

Hope International, located in Hollywood, California, has a long, colorful history. In the early part of the twentieth century, it was known as the church of the stars. However, as the neighborhood became less affluent, the church began to go into decline. Finally the church offered Ed Carey the pastorate; it was a last-ditch effort to save an inner-city church that had twenty members, was $280,000 in debt, and was operating on a monthly cash flow of negative $3,000.

Ed agreed to take the pastorate on the condition that the church would focus on missions, both foreign and local. "Even if we need to have our services by candlelight because our power has been turned off, we will devote ourselves to missions," he told them. They agreed.

Seven years later, Hope International is thriving. It is now debt-free, has one hundred fifty members, and has started several new churches. Last year, the church gave 24 percent of its gross income to missions. What happened?

One Sunday morning as Pastor Ed drove to church, he saw people in the neighborhood lounging on their front porches. They didn't seem to be on their way to church anywhere—in fact, there was a noticeable lack of evangelical churches in the area. Most of the people Pastor Ed saw were first generation Armenian and Russian immigrants who spoke no English. He'd been told there were about one hundred thousand of these immigrants in the immediate Hollywood-Glendale area.

The following week, armed with a few Armenian phrases, Pastor Ed stopped the car and approached two men and a woman. He asked them if they'd like to learn English. "Yes, yes!" they responded with enthusiasm. He told them that, if they came by his office on Saturday mornings, he would teach them English.

The next Saturday, six immigrants showed up at Pastor Ed's office. The three he had originally invited took the liberty of bringing a few friends. One of them spoke broken

English, so they were able to communicate. That morning Pastor Ed taught them some standard greetings and a few simple words. They had fun and got to know each other a bit.

Next week, twelve people came: nine Armenians and three Russians. Pastor Ed was out of greetings, so he started teaching them words from the Bible's concordance. When he tried to communicate the word *grace*, the Russians were puzzled. They didn't have a parallel word in the Russian language, but they were excited by the concept.

In two months, the group grew to twenty people. Pastor Ed asked his students if they would be willing to meet at nine on Sunday mornings instead. He encouraged them to sit in on the eleven o'clock service and listen to gain more exposure to English. Most of them began attending the service. They didn't understand any of the message at first, but they loved the music and loved being included in the larger community.

As the English class grew to twenty-five people, Pastor Ed ran across an Armenian translator. The whole group sat in the balcony and the translator whispered an Armenian version of the message. When the group reached thirty, a Russian translator was found. They then started what they now call The Old World Church. The messages were translated aloud into both languages, and the services began attracting Romanian, Hungarian, and Czech immigrants, as well.

MEETING NEEDS

Pastor Ed learned about the culture as he went along. In order to better understand the people he was teaching, he subscribed to Armenian and Russian newspapers that had sections in English so he could keep up with current events in those countries. He worked to build relationships with the people. He learned some simple prayers in their languages, and the congregation would laugh with him over his pronunciation. They appreciated that he was trying so hard. The people are still learning English through the services, since everything is preached in both languages in turn.

As Pastor Ed continued to preach about grace, lives started changing and people began making commitments to follow Christ. The Old World Church has now grown to between 135 and 150 adults, and over 90 percent of those who attend have become Christians.

The needs of the community are great. The people are poor, and many of them are in the United States illegally. In addition to providing English lessons, Hope International helps people with their legal status and in obtaining green cards. The church also helps people ship packages back home and lets them make overseas phone calls from the church office during the Russian and Armenian holidays.

Hope International and The Old World Church now consider themselves sister churches. They share a building and host barbecues and other events together, but they remain separate churches. They each have their own leadership base and are meeting the needs of two different groups of people. For the first four years, Pastor Ed preached for both churches, but now an elder preaches at The Old World Church.

CREATING NEW OPPORTUNITIES

Hope International also shares its facilities with Korean and Spanish language churches, and it started an African-American church with strong roots in the recovery community, as well as a series of apartment churches. Many readers may have heard of house churches, but apartment churches will likely require an explanation.

Lower income apartments dominate the housing landscape in the neighborhood where Hope International is located. Traditional methods of evangelism tend to be ineffective due to the lack of trust people feel when a stranger knocks on their door. Surveying the situation, Pastor Ed had two ideas.

One was to go to the laundromats. One of the best ways to do evangelism is to go to where the people already are. People in the community don't own their own washers or dryers, so they go to laundromats. There they have time to talk.

Pastor Ed's other idea involved contacting apartment managers. The managers knew the needs of everyone in the building. They knew whose power was being shut off and who needed food. Pastor Ed explained to the managers that the church wanted to help, and the managers began sending people his way. In cases of domestic violence or a death in the family, the apartment managers told people who couldn't afford counseling to go to the church for help. Essentially, the managers became conduits of evangelism. When people came to them with needs, they were directed to the church.

The strategy worked. Not only did the church make contacts with those living in the apartments, but two managers agreed to let Hope International use their lobbies to hold Bible studies and start churches there. The trend caught on, and soon there were more apartment churches. As each one was established, the church would appoint a man or woman living in the apartment building to be the chaplain. Needs would then be channeled through the chaplain.

To increase his outreach, Pastor Ed moved into one of the most run-down apartment buildings and became a chaplain. He lives four or five days a week in the inner city in order to understand the lives of the people and be more effective at ministering to them. He recognized that he was working within another culture and considered the city his mission field. If he didn't go without hot water and live among the rats and the roaches, how would he be able to relate to the people in the community on Sundays?

This one church alone has found numerous ways to reach out to the community and start other churches. There are opportunities everywhere. Look around. Be creative. Search out the people who are not being reached. Anyone can do it: people who don't speak the same language, churches that are broke, even teenagers!

OVERCOMING INTERNAL OBSTACLES

One church was started by a youth group from Janesville, Wisconsin. The youth pastor wanted to help raise money for church planting and discussed the matter with the director of church planting for his district. The director asked him, "Why don't you do the whole thing? I'll guide your youth group through the research and the demographics and help with the recruitment of a planter."

The youth group took him up on his offer. They hung door flyers, conducted surveys, went on prayer walks, and met with people in the community. Once they had prepared the way, the youth group called the church planter.

If anyone can do it, what gets in the way? If we truly believe that more churches are needed to reach more people, what roadblocks and obstacles stop us from being churches that plant other churches?

Probably the most common obstacle is the belief that "We're just not ready yet." However—ironically—the earlier a church can dive into church planting, the easier it will be.

The best time to establish habits is when you're young. Churches that put off church planting for years often never get around to doing it at all or encounter great resistance when they try.

Very young churches, on the other hand, can be quite effective at church planting. Pastor Tom Nebel's church gave birth to a daughter church when it was just three years old and had a Sunday morning attendance of 125 people. In fact, the daughter church held its first public service on the mother church's third anniversary.

Another common, but less-often-stated, reason for not planting other churches is the belief that church planting efforts will damage the parent church. Pastors and other leaders often are concerned about losing people and diminishing their financial resources. We worry that focusing on church planting will leave less time and energy to devote to internal programs. We can also feel threatened, fearing that someone else will show us up by building a larger, more successful ministry.

Yet if we raise up, train, and send out another leader who surpasses our own ministry, what a reason to rejoice! We will have made a dramatic contribution to the kingdom.

And what are we training people for if not to send them out? What are we raising money for if it is not to be used for extending God's kingdom? Anything less is a waste of what God has given us. Just as we as individuals tithe, whole churches need to practice generous giving as well—joyfully sharing leaders, resources, and ministries so other churches can be planted. Out of what God gives us, we give part back to him, and yet somehow he still provides for our needs. Many pastors who have congregations active in church planting find that, when they give away people, God raises up even more to take their places.

A third common roadblock to church planting is simple complacency. Many churches fear change. We worry that church planting will hinder our fellowship. We become comfortable where we are and refuse to reach out, because reaching out might prove to be uncomfortable or awkward. How will we know what to do? What if we fail? It's much safer to stay with what we've always known.

SEEING FROM GOD'S PERSPECTIVE

As Christians, we are faced with the continual challenge of seeing the world from God's perspective. We are here on earth for only a very short period of time, and we have been given an urgent assignment. There will be plenty of time to recline at God's table in the kingdom and renew old friendships, but how much more blessed will that time be if we multiply those Christian friendships to the ends of the earth right now?

There is no denying that positive change is often difficult, but it can happen and is well-worth the sacrifice. When one pastor began initiating major changes at his church, six board members left. Yet what initially looked like a disaster was really an opportunity for new leadership to rise up to meet the challenge. Obstacles will arise, but with faith they can be overcome.

GETTING STARTED

Consider possible steps your church could take toward church planting. Develop a vision for church planting, and share it with your congregation. Set long-range goals, and determine some steps that can be taken now.

There are countless ways to be involved. Many churches

send out an apprentice to start a new church. Sometimes this apprentice is a leader who has been raised up and trained by the sending church; sometimes he or she is a person brought in from outside and then sponsored by the sending church. In other cases, churches have sent out groups of people to start a new church. One church in Indiana felt called to start a church in Pennsylvania. They sent a group of six people from their congregation to go and be part of a core team for the new church plant. This method works even better for church plants in the immediate area, as they do not have the added expense and difficulty of relocation.

Other churches have started church-planter training programs. One church that is currently in the process of buying a building has been specifically looking for a facility that would work well as a training center for new church planters.

Smaller churches often prefer to cooperate with other congregations to plant new churches by providing finances, resources, and prayer support. Even people and leadership can be contributed—it just depends on what each church has to offer.

Planting churches cross-culturally should also be considered as an option. Although special gifting is generally required to minister successfully in cross-cultural situations, you don't always have to travel very far to find those situations. Starting a church in another country is always a possibility, but most of us cross paths with people from other cultures on a daily basis. There are so many opportunities right around us. The mission field is in our own backyard.

POSSIBILITY THINKING

Whatever you do, don't think too small. God wants to

bless you beyond your wildest dreams and bring in a harvest beyond what you can even imagine. Sometimes it's easier to see the obstacles than the possibilities. You don't need to know every step it will take to get from here to there; you just need to know where God wants you to go and to commit to following the vision he's given you.

To return to Hope International—what happened? How did a dying church sunk deep in debt become so revitalized and alive in just seven years? The key to revitalization lies in becoming outward-focused. The congregation at Hope International mobilized to help reach an end that was greater than itself. Members were no longer maintaining the status quo; they were reaching out toward a higher goal. The excitement of such endeavors is contagious, and the congregation came back to life. Paradoxically, inner health comes by pouring energies outward. Keep giving and giving—whether it's money, resources, or people.

When asked what advice he has for other pastors and church leaders who desire revitalization, Ed Carey responds, "Just keep loving people. That's all you really need. Love the unlovable. Touch the untouchable. Remember the kindness the Lord showed us when we were yet sinners, and we will be compelled to reach out. Outreach means reaching out—and not so you can bring it back in."

Endnotes

1. Christian Schwarz, *Natural Church Development*, (Carol Stream, IL: ChurchSmart Resources, 1996), 46-48.

ABOUT THE AUTHOR

Robert E. Logan, founder and executive director of CoachNet, Inc., is an internationally recognized authority in leadership development and church growth, as well as a strategist in establishing and multiplying new churches. He received his Doctor of Ministry in Church Growth at Fuller Theological Seminary and his Master of Divinity in Pastoral Ministries at Western Baptist Seminary. Dr. C. Peter Wagner, renowned expert on church growth and prayer, says, "Bob Logan is America's foremost authority in the field of church planting."

Seeing Beyond Church Walls

BE THERE

Leadership That Sees Beyond Church Walls

BY LEONARD SWEET

n Tina Sinatra's biography of her father, Frank Sinatra, she pays the chairman of the board the ultimate tribute. Her dad was "like a campfire, the point where we gathered and felt warm. He had such a big presence...When he was with you he was really *with* you."[1]

What's the greatest compliment anyone can receive? "Thanks for...being there."

These two words, *be there*, define the essence of the Incarnation, the centerpiece Christian doctrine in the Eastern Orthodox tradition. *Be* refers to character. *There* refers to context. *Be* is face. *There* is place. To *be there* is to know your face ("Who am I? What am I here for?") and know your place ("Where am I? What is to be done?"). To *be there* is to get your act together and to get other people together: to know Christ and to make Christ known.

In some ways, character and context do more than play off one another; they oppose one another. But it is the essence of incarnational theology that leadership exhibits this double loyalty—to be true both to one's unique identity as a disciple of Christ and, at the same time, to be true to one's unique cultural context. When character and context are in harmony, remarkable things can happen.

Character is destiny.
—Heraclitus

BE

Be is the issue of character. Do you know who you are, why you're here, what is the mission of your life?

I hail from mountain culture: My father was born in the foothills of the Adirondack Mountains, and my mother was born in the Allegheny Mountains. Part of being a product of the mountains is bracing each fall for the tourists—"leaf peepers" we called them—whose annual rite of lifting up their eyes unto the hills to see the leaves turn colors was as humorous to us "homies" as it was essential to our economic survival.

The truth is that leaves don't turn colors in the fall. As the days grow shorter, the trees stop manufacturing chlorophyll, which covers up the "true colors" of the leaves—bashful yellows, bold oranges, arrest-me reds, hide-and-seek russets.

Leaders with character let their true colors show. When the chlorophyll of conventions and civilities and coded conduct no longer is pumping, what shows?

What's your true color?

"The great tests of life reveal character. It is not until winter comes that we know the pine is an evergreen."
—Old English gravestone

Of course, our true colors are rooted and located in place. Face and place, character and context overlap in complex and mystifying ways. To some degree, "Where are you?" even comes before "Who are you?" Kentucky farmer/poet/philosopher Wendell Berry has made a career of reminding us that "If you don't know where you are, you don't know who you are." Just as "good poems come from roots" (John Haines wrote these words in the '70s), good persons come from roots as well.

Without strong roots, our faces can quickly become farces. "The first duty in life is to be as artificial as possible," Oscar Wilde wrote sarcastically. "What the second duty is no one has yet discovered." The Phillips translation of Romans 12:2 reads, "Do not let the world squeeze you into its mold." That word *world* could be crossed out and *church* inserted without distorting the intent of the author. The church opposes biological cloning but practices spiritual cloning with particular relish and finesse.

God created each one of our faces to be an original. William Blake, who in a despairing hour complained, "O why was I born with a different face?" then went on to answer his own question:

"The apple tree never asks the beech how he shall grow: nor the lion, the horse, how he shall take his prey... The eagle never lost so much time as when he submitted to learn of the crow."

Many of our faces look like following Jesus is more a life

sentence than a lifestyle. That's because we're trying to wear someone else's face instead of our own. We're afraid of being called the best thing anyone could ever call us: a character. How many people would be complimented being called a character? That's because leaders today are lightly character-ized. Character-ized leadership—that is, leadership based on character that is rooted in identity, integrity, and ideals—wears an original, one-of-a-kind face.

To be nobody but yourself in a world which is doing its best, night and day, to make you everybody else, means to fight the hardest battle which any human being can fight; and never stop fighting.
—e e cummings

The only face leaders are to wear other than our own is the face of Christ. Our "be-ings" are shaped by all sorts of things. In western culture, we most often construct our self, our be-ing, from the consuming culture. Buying an identity—"the commodity self"—is what most people mean by the word *style*. In many ways, ours *be-ings* are a compilation of our favorite brands and bands.

In contrast, the Christian *be-ing* is formed, reformed, and transformed by the character of Christ. But the more we become like Christ, the more we put on the mind of Christ, the more we morph into the face the Christ, the more unique our faces become. Christian *be-ing* is not an abandoning of identity but a turning toward God and an indwelling by God that enhances our identity and uniqueness. You become more *you*, more unique, more original, the more you become like Christ.

We can't show ourselves our own face or tell ourselves our own story. We need others to show us our face and tell us our story. Most importantly, we need God to reveal to us our own face and tell us our own story. That's why story-telling is a communal and interactive event. We can't see our own face or understand our own story until other people interact with our face and story. Until our story is connected to God's story, until our being is in a state of openness to God's being and to the fullness of being, there can be no true Christian character.

To be sure, character is transformed by action. Character is not infused in us magically by the Spirit. It takes practice; it takes discipline. It takes habits that become habitations. But there is something absolutely grace-full that takes place when our be-ing takes on the being of Christ.

I can't seem to get out of the book of Colossians in general, and this one verse in particular: "Christ in you, the hope of glory" (1:27b). Maybe it's the same reason eighteenth century evangelist George Whitefield couldn't stop preaching on the text, "Ye must be born again." When people asked Whitefield why he preached so often on this one passage, "Ye must be born again," he replied, "Because, ye must be born again!" The Incarnation is not something that just happened once. The Incarnation is something that happens in each one of us. It is not enough to hear the angels sing, "For *unto* you is born a Savior, Jesus Christ the Lord." Having the character of a Christian is to hear "For *in* you is born a Savior, Jesus Christ the Lord." Jesus is not a *product that works*. Jesus is not an *absolute principle*. Jesus is a *Person who is Real*, a *Divine Presence* that is *True and Indwelling*. Jesus is the *Infallible, Inerrant Word-Made-Flesh-and-Dwells-Among-Us Image of God*.

I want to be me without making it difficult for you to be you.
—Howard Thurman

In her collection of poems called *Evening Train*, poet Denise Levertov quotes an ex-slave:

> *I sits here, in my rocker, evenin's,*
> *and just*
> *purely*
> *be's.*

At the end of the poem, Levertov wrote,

> *...as the task before me, to be,*
> *to arrive at being.*[2]

The ultimate task in life is *to be* and to *arrive at being*.

> *People get ready, there's a train a comin';*
> *You don't need no baggage; you just get on board.*
> —Curtis Mayfield

THERE

The scandal of Incarnation is that God sanctifies each cultural setting as a site for the divine birth. Leaders are those who immerse their character in the context of which they are a part.

Leaders don't stand apart from culture and then reach down with ice tongs to pick it up. Leaders must be in their context and love their context. Leaders know the microclimate of the weather patterns (intellectual, social, political, and scientific) in which they live, not to the end of Christ transforming culture but to the end of Christ transforming persons and communities in every culture. The worst state for a church touched by God's love to be in is a church...*out of touch*.

I think it is possible to speak of the church today being in the midst of a "there" psychosis. A "there" psychosis is worse than denial. Denial is not taking your medicine. Some studies put the figure as high as 50 percent of patients who don't take the medications their doctors prescribe. A good number don't even bother to fill their prescriptions. The medical world calls this "noncompliance." It poses, one official says, "a huge problem larger than anyone imagines."[3]

When you're in denial, you put in the back of your mind the truth. You just don't want to face it. Denial is neurotic. The difference between a neurotic and a psychotic is this: psychotics believe that 2+2=5; neurotics know that 2+2=4, but they don't like it. When you're in psychosis, you actually convince yourself that something is truth that isn't.

What do psychotics do? They impose their fancies and fantasies on others. They persuade themselves that Julia Roberts really loves them, that John Lennon wants to kill them, or that something else is true that really isn't. Or in the case of a "there" psychosis, that it's not really a different world out there, and that the world that we feel most comfortable in is the world that we're really living in.

It's one thing for someone to live and never realize, or deny, the fundamental changes taking place during his or her lifetime. The masses of people do that. But it's another thing to call yourself a leader and not be there.

I don't want to wear rose-tinted glasses. But we in the church are wearing black-out shades. There's no *there* in most of our churches. The *there* that isn't *there* is the *there* that is the buzz of almost every academic discipline, every sector of society, except the church. Leaders are charged with an EPIC task: to put their face, not their back to the future. Here's one example of the *place* that's being *faced* by virtually every cultural context except the church:

"From any standpoint, it's clear the world is at something of a historical dividing line—the end of the modern era that began in the 1500s; the end of the Industrial Age; the end of America's population and culture being drawn primarily from Europe; the end of the monopoly of the printed word as the dominant mode of communication; the end of the Atlantic-based economic, political and military global hegemony; the end of the colonial period; the end of the nation-state as the outer limits of a people's identity; the end of the masculine, hierarchical epoch; and, as some have suggested, perhaps the end of the Christian eon. We're in what the ancient Greeks called *kairos*—the 'right moment' for a fundamental change in principles and symbols."[4]

There's a lot of *there* that I don't like or understand. As an academic trained in a Gutenberg curriculum and context, it is somewhat mortifying to learn that there is now at Washington State University a Taco Bell Distinguished Professor of Hotel and Restaurant Administration. There is now at Stanford University (no slouch school) a Yahoo! Chair of Information Systems Technology. The Georgia Institute of Technology now has a Coca-Cola Chaired Professor in its School of Industrial and Systems Engineering.

No matter how bizarre or off-putting "there" is, outward-focused leaders are those who will *be there* for the world in which God has placed them. There have been three great reinventions of education in the history of learning: 1) invention of the Greek alphabet in the eighth century B.C.; 2) invention of the printing press in the fifteenth century; 3) invention of the Web in the late twentieth, early twenty-first century.

Every leader, every church can *be there* in varying degrees. Not too long ago, I worshipped where I thought I would find traditional worship at its highest and finest. It had been a rough week, with all sorts of intellectual and spiritual skirmishes with leaders who oppose screen culture and attack people like me for "dumbing down the gospel."

One pastor told me that if he insisted on a screen in his church's sanctuary and moved to more EPIC models of ministry, he would lose his church. My soul felt like it needed a bath, and my brain a sauna. So I decided to immerse my being in worship where tradition is most cherished and preserved: St. Patrick's Cathedral in New York City.

Guess what I discovered during high mass at St. Patrick's Cathedral, the very residence of the Pope when he is in the United States! Screens, screens, and more screens. In fact, I counted ten screens—and those were just the ones I could see from where I was sitting. At least twice that number were scattered throughout the sanctuary and nestled in the statuary.

Whatever your character, whatever your context, *be there*. And in a more postmodern version of those two words *be there*,[5] say,

I'm in!

ENDNOTES

1. Tina Sinatra, *My Father's Daughter: A Memoir* (New York: Simon & Schuster, 2000), 45.

2. Denise Levertov, "Dream Instruction," *Evening Train* (New York: New Directions, 1993), 60-61.

3. Connie Lauerman, "More Patients Are Ignoring What Their Doctors Order," Charlotte Observer (25 December, 2000).

4. William Van Dusen Wishard, "A New Era of History," *Vital Speeches,* LXVII (1 December 2000), 104-110, 105.

5. With thanks to Steve Sallee, Senior Pastor of Cokesbury United Methodist Church, Knoxville, Tennessee, for this modulation of *be there* to *I'm in.*

About the Author

Dr. Leonard Sweet is a visionary and futurist who challenges thousands of church leaders at scores of conferences around the world each year. Holding an M.Div. degree from Colgate Rochester University and a Ph.D. from the University of Rochester, Dr. Sweet currently serves as the E. Stanley Jones Professor of Evangelism at Drew Theological School in Madison, New Jersey. He is the author of more than fifteen books, including AquaChurch, in which he details how church leaders must adapt to minister effectively in today's changing culture. In addition, Dr. Sweet is a key contributor to a Web site (www.preachingplus.com) that provides a wide range of worship and preaching resources for pastors.

LEADING FROM THE FRONT

Tips for Taking Your Church Beyond Its Walls

BY STEVE SJOGREN

he image of a true leader is powerfully shown in the 1964 film, *The Gospel According to St. Matthew* by Italian director Pier Paolo Pasolini (himself a Communist). Lesslie Newbigin comments on the film:

> *It shows Jesus going ahead of his disciples, like a commander leading troops into battle. The words he speaks are thrown back over his shoulders to the fearful and faltering followers. He is not like a general who sits at headquarters and send his troops into battle...He enables and encourages them by leading them, not just by telling them. In this picture, the words of Jesus have a different force. They all find their meaning in the...words, "Follow me."*[1]

LEADING OR PROMOTING

In his article "Getting Beyond the Numbers Game," James F. Engel describes a gathering of thousands of delegates from nearly two hundred countries for the second world congress of the Great Commission Council. As he opens the proceedings of this imaginary council, the chief missiologist announces that the Great Commission will be fulfilled within the lifetime of most of the people there. With great flourish, he produces statistics and computerized maps to describe how successfully the message is being spread.

Engel goes on to describe an African delegate who comes to the microphone and explains that she's from the country considered by many to be the greatest example of missionary success. She tells the audience "how the church was planted over a century ago and how today 85 percent of the people call themselves Christian." But other numbers tell another story. The delegate is from Rwanda where, "in 1994, six hundred thousand Tutsis and four hundred thousand Hutus died, many of them slaughtered with machetes as they huddled in churches."

" 'In all of your zeal for evangelism, you brought us Christ *but never taught us how to live.*' "[2]

With the development of a truly outwardly focused church come challenges to the structure of that church. Leadership isn't so much taught as it is caught. "My people become what I am." Our strategy must start with the raising up of small group apprentices and end with the grooming of leaders who embody the heartbeat of the outward-focused church.

PERSISTENCE, HOPE, AND RISK

Michael Essany understands persistence. He's the host of a half-hour public-access cable talk show. The comedian

Carrot Top told Time magazine that he was surprised when he showed up to be a guest on The Michael Essany Show and found himself in the living room of a three bedroom house in Valparaiso, Indiana. That's where Essany, a home-schooled eighteen-year-old, lives with his parents, an engineer and a homemaker. Carrot Top told Time magazine, "we walk into the house, and there in the living room was a TV studio!"

According to the young talk show host, the weekly show, which reaches 175,000 homes in Indiana and Illinois, is "boot camp. 'I'm getting all this experience here on the local level… which will help me when I get *The Tonight Show*. And I am going to host *The Tonight Show.*' " Since the show's inception in 1998, Essany has reeled in—by phone or in person—celebs as diverse as Ray Romano, Jenny McCarthy, Jim Nabors, Ed McMahon, Alex Trebek, and Deborah Norville." He's also been rejected hundreds and hundreds of times.[4]

Stepping Out Ahead of the Details

Each year a million-plus students take the SAT, the standard aptitude test required by many colleges, but only a handful will attain a perfect score. Rare as the perfect scores are, rarer still is a perfect score achieved by someone dealing with the adverse life situation that Trevor Loflin has faced. Much of the past two years, his pediatrician mother has been home-schooling him—but not at home. The family lost its traditional home through a series of financial difficulties, so they've been staying in their well-worn Chevy Suburban or camping out in tents in Northern California. Dinner usually consists of beans cooked over a small propane stove. What are Trevor's plans? Initially he plans to attend a Christian college to develop his character; later he plans to study astrophysics at California Institute of Technology.[3]

Why is he doing all of this? Because he wants to prove he's tenacious? Just to be on cable access TV? No. He has a goal. And he's persistent. In the three years since he started his show, he's asked one thousand people to be on his weekly program. At the top of his guest wish list: Jay Leno. Look out Jay. "When his time is through," says Essany, "That desk is mine."

OBSTACLES TO OUTWARDNESS

Roger Rosenblatt's little book titled *Rules for Aging* is filled with wisdom on how to live an outward life. For example, there's Rule #1: It Doesn't Matter; Rule #2: Nobody Is Thinking About You; Rule #3: Let Bad Enough Alone; Rule #5: Boo Yourself Off the Stage; Rule #8: If Something Is Boring You, It Is Probably You; Rule #15: Pursue Virtue, But Don't Sweat It; and Rule #42: The Unexamined Life Lasts Longer.[5]

Humorous and thought-provoking as these "rules" may be, they are all, in my opinion, an extension of my grandma's philosophy on life, a philosophy she shared with me as she approached her mid-eighties. As I watched her age and outlive a number of husbands, I watched her come into her own. It was almost as if she found a second adolescence in her eighties. Her comment: "I've gotten to the point in life where I really don't care much about what others think of me any longer. I feel tremendous liberty. *I recommend you get there as quickly in life as you can.*"

RULES FOR BECOMING OUTWARD

Get jazzed!

When was the last time you said, "Wow"? Before I

became a Christian, I used the expression *Wow!* frequently. I would say it many times a day. Somehow after I came to know the Lord and began to hang around the church scene, the sense of wonder about life began to diminish. At first reading, the Bible was thrilling and exciting, and I said *Wow!* quite often. But then I became familiar with the message of Scripture and accustomed to well-intentioned people explaining "what it really meant." The longer I've lived as a Christian, the more people have voluntarily appeared to remove virtually all aspects of mystery from the Christian life. It's no wonder that I slowly stopped uttering *Wow!*

During the past couple of years, I've sought to get impressed all over again with the simple things in life. I've made it a point to say *Wow!* at least a half dozen times a day. Sometimes people say, "You're kind of old to be saying *wow*, you know." To that I simply say, "Really? Wow!" I'm determined to get excited—frequently. And I'm committed to spreading that excitement to as many around me as possible. There's no overflow of excitement in the church these days.

Start saying *Wow!* a couple of times every day for practice. Look up from this book right now and utter a therapeutic *Wow!* right now. (If you're on an airplane people will wonder what you're up to!) Do it morning and evening for good measure. Aspire to be a little less sophisticated and a little more excited.

Change the world

From early on in life, I was interested in changing the world. When, at the age of seven, I heard John F. Kennedy announce the formation of the Peace Corps, I told my mom that I was going to join up when I got old enough. Then a most unexpected source encouraged my thinking in that direction a bit later in life.

When I was a senior in high school, I was in the midst of

massive rebellion against any sort of organized authority figure. I had long hair and was passionate about life. Then, while swimming with friends, I nearly drowned in an Arizona lake. I began to think about what life is all about, what counts, what matters, and what doesn't. At about that time, my speech teacher said everyone in the class would have to write and deliver a persuasive speech about any topic.

Looking back, I remember that the first part of a famous Christian poem was resonating in my heart, though I didn't have words for it yet: "Only one life, 'twill soon be past…" After struggling for days to select a topic to be persuasive about, I confessed to my elderly speech teacher, "I want to change things; I just don't know what to change." For some reason, he suggested that I talk to the leader of the local Salvation Army unit who was trying to raise community awareness, as well as money. I met with Lieutenant Johnson and, although we were a contrast of images and value systems, I sensed that, deep down, this too was a man who was out to change the world. I wrote the best, most impassioned speech I could about changing the world. I quoted lots of anti-Christian sources, including author Albert Camus and philosopher Fredrich Nietzsche. I don't remember much of what I said, but the gist of it was: *Life is short. Live it out for something that will outlast you!*

The good lieutenant came to class the day I spoke and politely listened to me. I was anything but a product of the Salvation Army. We were quite a study in contrasts—he with his brass buttons and uniform and me with my tie-dyed shirts and long hair. But he saw something in me and recruited me that day to become a fund-raiser with him. We began to travel around together to civic groups. He would show slides of what his group was doing, and I would give my "Life Is Short" speech. I don't remember just how many places the lieutenant and I spoke at, but the number was in the dozens. I suspect some thought he was going to introduce me as one of his halfway house graduates. Surely they were shocked when the conservative, clean-cut Christian man introduced Steve, the deadhead kid.

That was almost thirty years ago now. A couple of years after my speaking tour, while in college, I came to know Christ. Until recently I never connected the two events. Now I think the lieutenant was a good and very wise fellow. He saw in me something that is inherent in the heart and attitude of many not-yet Christians—*a desire to live for a cause that is beyond themselves.*

I want to hang out with people who are excited about life. I meet fewer and fewer Christians, it seems, who are excited. We're cautious, fearful, worried about getting into extremes, and all the while losing any semblance of edge that we possess. It's our edge that makes us attractive to the world around us.

Become useful

We must always pursue a practical living out of our outwardness. We are outward in deed, not in intent, or we are kidding ourselves.

Take small steps

My testimony is: "I'm not good, but I'm a lot better than I used to be. I'm making progress." I'm one of the few in the world who have survived a double aorta piercing! (I suffered a severe medical mishap a few years ago that affected neurology throughout my body). Surviving that accident is amazing to begin with. I reflect a little bit on that every day of my life when the going gets tough—every day is a tough day for me now. But I've learned to measure life in small, incremental steps. That's not only realism for me, it's good for the soul. It's the way forward when we are seeking to shift to an outward-focused church.

Hang out with people who believe in you and your vision

Be careful about the company you keep. Limit the time you spend with vision detractors. Any time you are seeking to bring a new idea to the fore, your fair share of critics will be standing nearby. Guaranteed.

Some of us need to cut ourselves off from some of our present friends because they aren't a positive influence on our vision and dream life. Detractors take enormous amounts of energy and time. We often get used to their presence and energy-draining effect the way we get used to a whining refrigerator that needs replacing.

After the initial idea has been introduced and a reasonable amount of explanation has been offered to reasonable people, I have to limit the amount of time I spend each day dealing with detractors. I set a time limit of, say, fifteen minutes. When that time has been eaten up, I inform those I'm with that I have already talked myself out on that issue for the day and could we talk about that tomorrow or the next day for fifteen minutes. It's wise to put a time limit on discussion. Some people have an unquenchable thirst for oppositional attitudes. No matter what you attempt to do, there will always be detractors.

Even Mother Teresa, in spite of her cherished place in most hearts, was no stranger to criticism. A number of critical books have been written about Mother Teresa, the most famous of which is entitled *The Missionary Position* by Christopher Hitchens. The author questions the motives of virtually every word and action of the good mother's public ministry.[7] She was just a human, but she did some pretty spectacular things on earth just the same. To quote nineteenth century evangelist Dwight Moody, "I like what I'm doing better than what you aren't doing."

Are We Clear on Who Our Leaders Are?

In the UK, the royal mail ran a survey to discover who were the most admired "mums" in the world. When it comes to celebrity mums, the most admired mum was Princess Diana, who received 28 percent of the vote. (She was killed in an auto accident in the company of the man with whom she was having a very public affair.) Mother Teresa came in second with 24 percent of the vote. Interestingly pop diva Madonna came in a close third with 21 percent of the vote.[8]

Don't worry about "impossibilities"

Keith Green wrote a song with the refrain "He'll take care of the rest." God is looking for available people who can dream and are willing to risk big. Sure, there is a practical side to all of this, but imagining all the barriers too early in the process can be overwhelming.

PRACTICE

Just start

Sometimes we are a little too results oriented.

Do a consistent outreach activity for at least six months before you begin to assess your results. It takes time to begin to see something worthwhile get started.

Look for small changes/advances/encouragements/ adventures

"Watch and pray" (Matthew 26:41a).

Jesus makes it clear—the kingdom of God comes bit by bit as we do the small things and look for change to take place.

Our house has an insect problem. We are inundated with the critters. They are present year-round, but in light of what they are my wife, Janie, and I can't bring ourselves to call the bug zappers. You see, *lady bugs* love our house! These little guys have slowly, surely grown on us. They've gone from being a bit of an imposition to welcome guests.

This is the way it works with outreach. Success goes to the ones who keep on keeping on.

Develop a vocabulary of change

A Christian author asked a friend of mine, "What do you think a definition of the gospel is?" My friend answered, "Repent and believe in Jesus for the forgiveness of your sins."

"Wrong," said the author. "The message of the gospel is this: Behold, the kingdom of God has come!"

The author was right. My friend's oversimplified answer, though it's the common understanding of the gospel, is just a portion of the overall message in the gospel of Jesus Christ. Jesus proclaimed the presence of the kingdom of God over and over.

Sometimes we have to marry the right words with the right concept to connect with people properly. If you don't explain in new words and images what you are doing and where you are headed, others will create words and images. Their words and images will be less gracious and accurate than yours.

When a small group becomes two groups, say, "We are multiplying"; never say, "We are dividing our group." When new folks come to your church, call them newcomers to immediately include them in the life of the congregation and make them part of the inclusive *us*. Don't call them visitors—a term that connotes that they are outsiders. When you talk about so-called "short-term missions" why not use something more creative and inclusive, such as, "serving vacations"?

Reinvent yourself and your group

Every group needs an occasional reinvention. After leading churches for over twenty years, I'm convinced that about every five years a local church needs a semi-significant reinvention. Then about every twenty years every church needs to be essentially restarted from the ground level up. By that I mean that religious form becomes so ingrained, so calcified, that a significant shake-up is absolutely necessary.

We need a regular reinvention in life, hopefully before we progress too far down the path.

A LIFE WORTH LIVING?

I'd seen people die before, plenty of times actually, but I'd never been with someone who died suddenly, violently. I was returning to Cincinnati on a Sunday evening Delta flight from Dallas that had maybe a dozen people spread throughout the plane. On this cold November evening,

Don't Take Yourself Too Seriously

St. Joseph's Hawks' Phil Martelli loves everything about college basketball except the clichés that his fellow coaches spout.

His Number One peeve?

"At the Final Four coaches convention, everybody has a sweat suit, and they all call each other 'coach,' " he said. "Everybody says 'coach,' and they whip their head around. It's like Linda Blair in *The Exorcist*."

Other annoyances? Teams that play hard. (Talk about intensity! "You're just playing basketball," says Martelli.)

Known for poking fun at himself and his sport, Martelli chides other coaches for taking themselves too seriously.[9]

nothing and no one seemed out of the ordinary until the guy sitting a row in front of me started to have difficulty swallowing his orange juice and vodka drink. The woman sitting next to him called the flight attendant, and together they must have concluded he was choking because they began to slap his back with so much gusto that all the contents of his pockets—shirt and pants—eventually spilled out onto the floor. But he just turned a darker shade of blue. Though a call went out for volunteers, there were no medical personnel onboard to help. As soon as we landed, emergency medical technicians rushed on the plane and applied the electroshock paddles to his chest. All that did was cause a bit of remaining change left in his pocket to fly out onto the aisle. After they carried him out, with a sheet over his face, it was eerie stepping over his things. Car keys, a pack of cigarettes, a Zippo lighter with a Corvette logo on it, and a dollar's worth of change were the things that represented his life on this earth.

As I stepped over this man's possessions, I wondered, "What would emergency workers zap out of my pockets?"

That's a question worth asking every once in a while. It's easy to get bogged down with nonessentials.

DREAM—DREAM B-I-G

Effective communication isn't just being a talking head; it's being a speaking-doing person. The greatest compliment given to me was by a lady who approached me with a rather suspicious look. She said, "I've been watching you. I've figured out what you are."

"Please tell me," I asked, "I've been trying to figure out what I am myself."

She said, "You're a speaking-doing person."

Based on the tone of her voice, I wasn't sure it was a compliment, but I decided to take it as a positive just the same.

Our audience isn't the Elk's Club, listening patiently for our speech concerning the upcoming fundraiser. It's the not-yet-Christian world that is dying to hear and experience a word from God. Just a single bit of evidence to convince them that God is real, authentic, and honest, and that God is for them. They have a dream of that sort of God in their heart. They are just waiting for us to show them some sort of evidence to confirm their dream. We all can be both dream fulfillers and dreamers.

We're All the Same Except for Our Dreams

As science unravels more information about the makeup of human DNA, it's turning out that we are a lot more alike than we are different. Time magazine noted that, for all of our differences in outward appearance, the differences are miniscule, according to the latest research. "We're all made from nearly identical building blocks," one foreign dignitary declared, "The day that discovery was made was a bad day indeed for racists and xenophobes."[10] So what's the difference between one person and another if it's not physical? Our dreams are what distinguish us from one another.

EVERYBODY HAS TO DREAM

I have a dream—of dancing one day. That may not sound like much of a dream, but considering my significant, permanent injuries, dancing is pretty much out of the question right now. In fact, just walking without the aid of a cane is hard to conceive.

To spur my dream along, I keep a photo in my office—it's the only one I keep. It's of Gene Kelly dancing. Actually, it's more like Gene Kelly leaping through the air in one of his movies. He must be more than three feet off the ground with a huge smile on his face. When people ask why I keep that photo around, I simply say, "Oh, that's a picture of me after the Lord heals my legs." Recently I morphed over Gene's face and replaced it with my own! I suspect his producer wouldn't appreciate my creativity (especially if I started selling these as postcards), but that's my dream. That's not where I am now. In fact, I'm far from it. I'm unable to feel my legs. I can't control the quadriceps muscles in my legs, which makes walking possible only with a cane. When I walk, I do so only with difficulty, and I move like an old man even though I'm in my mid-forties.

Still, I dream of dancing, of doing flying leaps to the glory of God just so I can explain to people, "This is impossible. I am supposed to be in a walker. But here I am leaping away. Go figure. To God be the glory."

Let's dream away and start to leap at the dream of becoming the outward-focused church. It's not where we are, but it's where we are headed, by the empowering of God.

Dream big. Dream out, not in. Behold, the kingdom of God is here!

ENDNOTES

1. Lesslie Newbigin, *The Gospel in a Pluralist Society* (Grand Rapids, MI: William B. Eerdmans Publishing Co., 1989), 230.

2. James F. Engel, "Getting Beyond the Numbers Game," Christianity Today, (August 7, 2000).

3. Eric Bailey, "Homelessness No Barrier for Honor Student and Teacher—His Mother," Los Angeles Times (8 April 2001), A32.

4. "Fresh Prince of Talk," Time magazine (2 April, 2001), p. 72.

5. Roger Rosenblatt, *Rules for Aging* (New York: Harcourt, 2001).

6. For a *Green Acres* fix complete with the theme song, check out www.maggiore.net/greenacres/.

7. Christopher Hitchens, *The Missionary Position: Mother Teresa in Theory and Practice* (New York: Verso, 1995).

8. "UK Mums Are Tops…Says Royal Mail Survey," PR Newswire Europe Limited, Universal News Service (21 March, 2001).

9. Beth Harris, "Martelli's Peeve is 'Coachspeak,' " AP Online (March 16, 2001).

10. "So, We've Got the Genome Map. Now, What to Do With It?," Time.com (February 13, 2001).

Group Publishing, Inc.
Attention: Product Development
P.O. Box 481
Loveland, CO 80539
Fax: (970) 669-1994

Evaluation for *Seeing Beyond Church Walls*

Please help Group Publishing, Inc., continue to provide innovative and useful resources for ministry. Please take a moment to fill out this evaluation and mail or fax it to us. Thanks!

● ● ●

1. As a whole, this book has been (circle one)

not very helpful   very helpful

1   2   3   4   5   6   7   8   9   10

2. The best things about this book:

3. Ways this book could be improved:

4. Things I will change because of this book:

5. Other books I'd like to see Group publish in the future:

6. Would you be interested in field-testing future Group products and giving us your feedback? If so, please fill in the information below:

Name _____

Street Address _____

City _____ State _____ Zip _____

Phone Number _____ Date _____

Flagship church resources

from Group Publishing

Innovations from Leading Churches

Flagship Church Resources are your shortcut to innovative and effective leadership ideas. You'll find ideas for every area of church leadership including pastoral ministry, adult ministry, youth ministry and children's ministry!

Flagship Church Resources are created by the leaders of thriving, dynamic and trend-setting churches around the country. These nationally recognized teaching churches host regional leadership conferences and are looked to for training by other pastors and church leaders due to their proven-effective approach to ministry. These resources reveal the proven ideas, programs and principles that these churches have put into practice!

Flagship Church Resources currently available:

- *Doing Life With God*
- *Doing Life With God 2*
- *The Visual Edge:*
  Compelling Video Connectors for Your Worship Experience
- *Mission-Driven Worship:*
  Helping Your Changing Church Celebrate God
- *An Unstoppable Force:*
  Daring to Become the Church God Had in Mind
- *A Follower's Life:*
  12 Group Studies on What It Means to Walk With Jesus
- *Leadership Essentials for Children's Ministry*
- *Keeping Your Head Above Water:*
  Refreshing Insights for Church Leadership
- *Seeing Beyond Church Walls:*
  Action Plans for Touching Your Community
- *unLearning Church:*
  Just When You Thought You Had Leadership All Figured Out!

With more to follow!

Exciting Resources for Pastors and Church Leaders

AquaChurch: Essential Leadership Arts for Piloting Your Church in Today's Fluid Culture

Leonard Sweet

In this latest and most accessible work from church historian, futurist and best-selling author Leonard Sweet, church leaders will discover the leadership arts that are essential in today's ever-changing culture. The author provides thought-provoking yet practical skills that will elevate the scope of ministry from mere survival of daily challenges to thriving in today's culture! Rather than provide new maps that will soon be obsolete, this book illustrates the need to become an "AquaChurch" in order to effectively minister in a fluid, postmodern culture. ISBN 0-7644-2151-4

The AquaChurch Challenge: Leadership Video Training Kit

Leonard Sweet

This dynamic video training kit will both captivate and inform your entire leadership staff. You'll loose the incredible creative potential within your team and help set the course for your church for years to come. Includes the Training Video, Leader Guide, Overhead Transparencies and a copy of the AquaChurch book. ISBN 0-7644-2226-X

Experience God in Worship

Discover the look of worship in the 21st century! Find out what thriving churches are doing, what changes they're planning, and how your church can make worship a joyful celebration all year long! You'll hear from nationally recognized authorities *George Barna, Gary M. Burge, Richard Allen Farmer, Jack W. Hayford, Kim Hill, Bruce H. Leafblad, John S. Miller, Leonard Sweet,* and *Robert Webber.* Whether your church is evangelical, African-American, liturgical, charismatic, contemporary or something in-between, you'll gain insight into current trends, lasting traditions, and more. ISBN 0-7644-2133-6

An Unstoppable Force: Daring to Become the Church God Had in Mind

Erwin Raphael McManus

Be inspired about being part of the Church God had in mind—a "force" created to change the world. A Church free from atrophied practices, flourishing in creative and compelling worship, reaching out to the community with "outside the box" expressions of love and faith. ISBN 0-7644-2306-1

Lost in America: How You and Your Church Can Impact the World Next Door

Tom Clegg & Warren Bird

Packed with compelling statistics, Lost in America will challenge the way you think about evangelism—and give you a soul-stirring new vision for what it can be. Includes practical advice and options for applications to evangelism in your church. ISBN 0-7644-2257-X